谨以此书献给我最挚爱的师长、学生与同仁！
To My Dearest Teachers, Students & Colleagues!

黄金葵
Huang Jinkui

新理念旅游英语情景听说

（第2版）

New Concept English for Tourism:
Scenario-based Listening & Speaking

（Second Edition）

黄金葵　编　著

清华大学出版社
北京交通大学出版社
·北京·

内容简介

《新理念旅游英语情景听说》是为大学通识教育课程体系专门开发的教材，可供中高级英语学习者使用。它和《经典旅游景观导游词赏析与口译》是姊妹篇，亦可用作旅游院校专业英语课程的配套教材。

本书共分为八个单元。情境导入模块包括机场服务、膳宿服务、餐饮服务、购物服务、旅行咨询与预订、游程商定、现场导游1、现场导游2。文化阐释模块包括常用旅游目的地、酒店文化、中国饮食文化、纪念品、祥瑞动植物、传说与人物掌故、传统节日、传统服饰与中国戏曲。作业任务模式包括情景小品表演和单句口译。

本书封面贴有清华大学出版社防伪标签，无标签者不得销售。
版权所有，侵权必究。侵权举报电话：010-62782989　13501256678　13801310933

图书在版编目（CIP）数据

新理念旅游英语情景听说/黄金葵编著. —2版. —北京：北京交通大学出版社：清华大学出版社，2020.9
ISBN 978-7-5121-3473-7

I.①新… Ⅱ.①黄… Ⅲ.①旅游—英语—听说教学 Ⅳ.①F59

中国版本图书馆CIP数据核字（2017）第330255号

新理念旅游英语情景听说
XINLINIAN LÜYOU YINGYU QINGJING TINGSHUO

策划编辑：郭东青
责任编辑：郭东青
出版发行：清 华 大 学 出 版 社　　邮编：100084　　电话：010-62776969
　　　　　北京交通大学出版社　　邮编：100044　　电话：010-51686414
印 刷 者：艺堂印刷（天津）有限公司
经　　销：全国新华书店
开　　本：203 mm×280 mm　印张：14.5　字数：450千字
版 印 次：2012年9月第1版　2020年9月第2版　2020年9月第1次印刷
印　　数：1～2 000册　定价：39.90元

本书如有质量问题，请向北京交通大学出版社质监组反映。对您的意见和批评，我们表示欢迎和感谢。
投诉电话：010-51686043，51686008；传真：010-62225406；E-mail：press@bjtu.edu.cn

Preface 第2版前言

旅游教育是21世纪高等院校通识教育的重要组成部分。《新理念旅游英语情景听说》是为大学通识教育课程体系专门开发的教材,可供中高级英语学习者使用。它和《经典旅游景观导游词赏析与口译》是姊妹篇,亦可用作旅游院校英文导游讲解技能训练的配套教材。

本书共分八个单元,每单元均由情境导入、文化阐释和作业任务三个模块构成。在任务设计方面始终贯穿3个教学理念:(1)充分利用现代化多媒体教学技术展现真实的导游工作场景。(2)强调对异域文化风情的深度解读,培养学生的团队合作精神。(3)突出口语、翻译、写作等产出型语言能力的培养。

一、情境导入模块。该模块提供真实情景听力。本书的全部听力录音均以多媒体课件的形式提供给读者,使得教学效果更加直观。所有听力课文均选编自英语国家教材,场景生动逼真,题材新颖广泛,充分体现了本书的国际化视野。

二、文化阐释模块。(1)词汇识记。旅游英语的词汇教学是一个非常关键的环节,然而,其体系之庞大,内容之繁多,常常令学生望而却步。为此,我们特别设计了图文并茂的热身游戏,寓教于乐,让学生在课堂游戏中领略旅游英语世界的奥妙。(2)小组项目。这是小组合作学习的最高形式,也是学生最有成就感的练习项目。本书结合中国旅游业的实际工作场景设计了趣味新颖的口语研讨项目,并配置了详细的任务工作表和辅助提示信息,颇具创新性。

三、作业任务模块。该模块提供情景小品表演和单句口译。在作业设计上,前六个单元为小组情景小品表演。随着学习者英文熟练度和精确度的提高,最后两个单元为单句口译任务,这和后续教材《经典旅游景观导游词赏析与口译》中的任务要求充分衔接,以便学习者顺利过渡。

此外,本书在附录中提供小组项目研讨会素材一套,情景小品口试样题两套,各单元课后练习答案,课程评价说明,情景听力音频将以电子教参的形式挂在网上。欢迎广大教师根据任教班级的实际教学情况、地方旅游景区的具体特点及学生的现实英语需求，在授课时对教学内容与形式进行灵活调整与改编，也诚挚地希望各位读者对本书提出宝贵意见。

编　者
2019 年 8 月

前 言

Preface

旅游教育是 21 世纪高等院校通识教育的重要组成部分。《新理念旅游英语情景听说》是为大学英语通识教育课程体系专门开发的教材,可供中高级英语学习者使用。它和《经典旅游景观导游词赏析与口译》是姊妹篇,亦可用作旅游院校专业英语课程的配套教材。

本教材在任务设计方面贯穿了三个新颖的教学理念:(1)最大限度地利用现代化多媒体教学技术展现真实的交际场景;(2)强调通过以小组为单位进行活动,培养学生的团队意识和合作探索精神;(3)突出口语、写作、翻译等产出型语言能力的终极培养。本书共分八个单元,每单元均包括情景听力任务和口语小组项目讨论任务。每单元分为如下三个模块。

一、听力模块:真实情景听力。本教材的全部听力录音均以多媒体课件的形式提供给读者,使得教学效果更加直观。所有听力录音均选编自国外教材,场景生动逼真,题材新颖广泛,充分体现了本教材的国际化视野。

二、口语模块:(1)专业词汇热身。旅游英语的词汇教学是一个非常关键的环节,然而,其体系之庞大,内容之繁多,常常令许多学生望词生畏。为此,我们特别设计了图文并茂的词汇识记热身游戏,寓教于乐,让学生在课堂词汇识记游戏中领略旅游英语世界的奥妙。(2)小组项目研讨。这是小组合作学习的最高形式,也是学生最有成就感的练习项目。本教材结合中国旅游业的实际工作场景设计了趣味新颖的口语研讨项目,并配置了详细的任务工作表和辅助提示信息,颇具创新性。

三、作业模块:情景小品表演或段落口译。在作业设计上,前六个单元为小组情景小品表演,随着学习者英文熟练度和精确度的提高,最后两个单元为段落口译任务,这和后续教材《经典旅游景观导游词赏析与口译》中的任务要求充分衔接,以便学习者顺利过渡。

此外，本教材在附录中提供期末小组项目研讨会样题一套，情景小品口试样题两套，各单元课后练习答案及课程评价说明，供教师参考使用。本书除听力练习选编自国外教材外，其余全部内容均为作者原创。在实际教学中，欢迎广大教师根据任教班级的实际教学情况、地方旅游景观的实际特点及学生的实际英语水平，在授课时对教学内容与形式进行灵活调整与改编，也诚挚地希望各位读者对本书提出宝贵意见。

编　者

2012 年 8 月

Contents

Unit 1 1

    Scenario Warm-up 1 Airport Service.. 3

    Culture Interpretation 1 Popular Destinations 8

    Assignment 1 Role-play Tasks 15

Unit 2 17

    Scenario Warm-up 2 Accommodation... 19

    Culture Interpretation 2 Hotel Culture... 37

    Assignment 2 Role-play Tasks 55

Unit 3 57

    Scenario Warm-up 3 Catering 59

    Culture Interpretation 3 Chinese Cuisine... 63

    Assignment 3 Role-play Tasks 71

Unit 4 75

    Scenario Warm-up 4 Shopping.. 77

    Culture Interpretation 4 Souvenir 81

    Assignment 4 Role-play Tasks 84

Unit 5 91

    Scenario Warm-up 5 Travel Inquiry & Booking................................ 93

    Culture Interpretation 5 Auspicious Fauna and Flora 111

    Assignment 5 Role-play Tasks 121

Unit 6 ·· 125

    Scenario Warm-up 6 Itinerary Negotiation 127

    Culture Interpretation 6 Folklores and Legendary Figures.......................... 139

    Assignment 6 Role-play Tasks 141

Unit 7 ·· 146

    Scenario Warm-up 7 Guiding Speech 1 147

    Culture Interpretation 7 Traditional Festivals... 154

    Assignment 7 Pair Interpretation Tasks 156

Unit 8 ·· 159

    Scenario Warm-up 8 Guiding Speech 2 161

    Culture Interpretation 8 Traditional Costumes & Chinese Operas 166

    Assignment 8 Pair Interpretation Tasks 176

Appendix ·· 177

    Appendix A Seminar Project 179

    Appendix B Role-play Test Paper 182

    Appendix C Key to Exercises 190

    Appendix D Course Assessment... 217

Bibliography ··· 219

Unit 1

Scenario Warm-up 1 Airport Service

Culture Interpretation 1 Popular Destinations

Assignment 1 Role-play Tasks

Scenario Warm-up 1 Airport Service

Listening Extract 1

Juliette Wilson works on the check-in desk at Sydney Airport. Listen to her checking in a passenger and answer the following questions.

1. Which of the following is the main problem: cancellation, lost ticket, overbooking, baggage, or unhelpful staff?

_____

2. What was the weight of the bag?

_____

3. Why does the passenger need the bag as the hand luggage?

_____

4. What solution does Juliette propose?

_____

5. Why is it important for him to get the first flight?

_____

6. Is overbooking illegal?

_____

7. What other solution does Juliette propose?

_____

8. What job does the woman with blonde hair do?

_____

9. What should the passenger do with his suitcase?

_____

Listening Transcript for Extract 1

(Courtesy of Strutt, English for International Tourism Intermediate Students' Book, Unit 9, Exercise 3: 138–139)

Juliette	Good morning. Do you have any luggage to check in?
Passenger	No, just the one piece of hand baggage.
Juliette	May I see, please?
Passenger	Sure.
Juliette	I'll just check the weight. I'm very sorry, it's 18 kilos, so I'll have to check it through. You won't be able to take it on board as hand baggage.
Passenger	But there's paperwork in there I need on the plane.
Juliette	OK, if you'd like to take some things out.
Passenger	I don't understand. This case was sold to me as cabin size.
Juliette	I'm sorry but you're only allowed 12 kilos on board and it's far too heavy. May I see your passport? I'm afraid you're on standby for the moment.
Passenger	What do you mean? I made this reservation three months ago. I have my ticket. I must leave on this flight.
Juliette	I understand but the flight has been oversold and as you're one of the last people to check in — I don't mean you're late — but unfortunately the airline has sold more tickets than there are seats on this flight.
Passenger	But that's illegal! It's your job to put me on this flight — I have an important meeting in Berlin and I can't miss it.
Juliette	I really understand how you feel but all airlines follow this policy. The only thing you can do is (to) wait until the end of check-in at 8:30. If you come back and see my colleague, the blonde-haired woman over there, then she'll call those who can leave by their names and give them their boarding passes. If no one calls you, just stay in front of the desk. That means you won't leave on that flight, unfortunately, but the

	supervisor will put you on the next flight and arrange compensation.
Passenger	So the blonde girl is the supervisor?
Juliette	No, not exactly. She's responsible for this flight and she's the one who'll call the supervisor who'll look after you.
Passenger	OK, but I'm not happy about this. And what about my case?
Juliette	I've put a security sticker on it and I'm giving it back to you. If we can put you on the next flight I'll take it back. If not, you'll have to check it in again for the next one.
Passenger	OK, I'll hang around.

Supplementary Reading Extract 1

Please read a tour guide speech on a shuttle bus from the airport to the resort.

Hello everyone,

My name is Luca. On behalf of Suntan Tours I'd like to welcome you all to Los Cabos. The bus ride to your hotel will take about fifteen minutes. Right now I'd like to take a minute to familiarize you with the area and discuss some brief safety precautions. Firstly, I ask that you remain seated until we reach our destination and that you not eat or drink while on the bus. Secondly, please realize that it is against the law to get drunk in public. Enjoy your vacation, but do drink responsibly and do not drink and drive.

I promise you are going to enjoy your stay here in San Jose, Los Cabos. This is a beautiful, quiet city where you can relax, sit by the beach, enjoy great meals and feel very safe. You can walk into town and enjoy the fountains or take a moonlit walk along the water. Please do not swim here. This is not a safe place to swim because there is a strong undertow. Cabos San Lucas is the place to go if you want to enjoy swimming in the ocean. You can take a short bus ride from your hotel. There you will also enjoy entertainment and dancing.

Suntan Tours offers a variety of special discounts depending on your travel plans. We have golf packages, as well as guided whale boat tours, and fishing charters. There will be a short information session at 1 p.m. in the lobby of the hotel tomorrow where you can learn all about these offers. We recommend that you do not purchase packages from street vendors as they are not always 100 percent reliable. They also may charge you more than what they say. Please take my advice and allow Suntan Tours to book all of your day trips and activities while you are here.

If you need to exchange your dollars into pesos, please use a bank or money exchange. We don't recommend exchanging your money at the hotel because you won't get a fair rate. Some restaurants will accept American or Canadian money, but you are better off to exchange your money and pay with pesos. Or, if you prefer, you can always use your credit cards. Also, if you want to get around the city, or travel to Cabos San Lucas, we recommend that you take the local bus rather than a taxi. The bus costs about one American dollar, and the driver can give you change if you don't have the exact amount. If you do decide to take a taxi, make sure that you negotiate a price before you go.

We're going to be pulling up to the hotel in just a few minutes. Please sit back and enjoy the view of the ocean on the left hand side of the bus as we enter the city. I ask that you remain in your seats until we have come to a complete stop. Javier will be meeting us at the bus to help you with your bags. Please double check to make sure your bag has been taken off the bus. On behalf of Suntan Tours, have a wonderful vacation in San Jose and I hope to see you tomorrow at the information session.

Please check your understanding by doing the following multiple-choice questions with your group members.

1. What does the tour guide say is illegal in Los Cabos?
    a) Drinking alcohol   b) Renting cars
    c) Being drunk in public   d) Standing on buses
2. What advice does the tour guide give about transportation?
    a) Have the correct change   b) Don't travel at night
    c) Tip the taxi drivers   d) Use public transit
3. Where are tourists recommended to exchange their money?
    a) At the hotel   b) On the bus
    c) At a bank   d) At the tour agency

> **Notes: Welcoming Procedure in Guiding Service**
> 1. *Contacting the escort*; 2. *Greeting the group*; 3. *Member confirming*;
> 4. *Luggage confirming*; 5. *Additional service*; 6. *Guiding to the coach.*

Culture Interpretation 1 Popular Destinations

Vocabulary Workshop

Are you familiar with the popular tourist destinations? Please tell your group members what their English equivalents are.

1. 新加坡	2. 泰国	3. 马来西亚	4. 菲律宾	5. 印度尼西亚
6. 韩国	7. 日本	8. 越南	9. 柬埔寨	10. 尼泊尔
11. 印度	12. 斯里兰卡	13. 马尔代夫	14. 文莱	15. 蒙古
16. 中国	17. 牙买加	18. 加拿大	19. 美国	20. 古巴
21. 墨西哥	22. 秘鲁	23. 巴西	24. 南非	25. 埃及
26. 新西兰	27. 澳大利亚	28. 挪威	29. 瑞典	30. 冰岛
31. 芬兰	32. 丹麦	33. 波兰	34. 捷克	35. 匈牙利
36. 俄罗斯	37. 德国	38. 瑞士	39. 奥地利	40. 法国
41. 卢森堡	42. 比利时	43. 荷兰	44. 英国	45. 爱尔兰
46. 土耳其	47. 葡萄牙	48. 西班牙	49. 意大利	50. 希腊
51. 东京	52. 京都	53. 大阪	54. 首尔	55. 新德里
56. 曼谷	57. 雅加达	58. 马尼拉	59. 开罗	60. 开普敦
61. 柏林	62. 慕尼黑	63. 法兰克福	64. 维也纳	65. 巴黎
66. 罗马	67. 威尼斯	68. 米兰	69. 苏黎世	70. 伯尔尼

71. 哥本哈根	72. 奥斯陆	73. 赫尔辛基	74. 雷克雅未克	75. 斯德哥尔摩
76. 雅典	77. 圣彼得堡	78. 莫斯科	79. 都柏林	80. 伦敦
81. 爱丁堡	82. 苏格兰	83. 曼彻斯特	84. 渥太华	85. 多伦多
86. 温哥华	87. 华盛顿	88. 纽约	89. 夏威夷	90. 洛杉矶
91. 旧金山	92. 波士顿	93. 芝加哥	94. 西雅图	95. 拉斯维加斯
96. 里约热内卢	97. 悉尼	98. 堪培拉	99. 墨尔本	100. 惠灵顿
101. 基督教	102. 天主教	103. 东正教	104. 大教堂	105. 大主教
106. 牧师	107. 耶稣基督	108. 梵蒂冈	109. 圣母	110. 三位一体
111. 教皇	112. 耶路撒冷	113. 管风琴/风琴/手风琴	114. 唱诗班/钢琴	115. 圣经
116. 穆斯林	117. 伊斯兰教	118. 麦加	119. 清真寺	120. 古兰经
121. 庙宇	122. 城堡	123. 祭坛	124. 宫殿	125. 陵寝
126. 纪念堂/纪念碑	127. 温泉/水疗	128. 雕塑/喷泉	129. 故居/别墅	130. 水坝/河堤/运河

续表

131. 大西洋	132. 北冰洋	133. 太平洋	134. 印度洋	135. 亚洲
136. 欧洲	137. 非洲	138. 北美洲	139. 南美洲	140. 大洋洲
141. 南极洲	142. 岛/屿	143. 半岛/群岛	144. 海角	145. 海湾
146. 彩虹	147. 瀑布	148. 高原/平原	149. 江河/溪流	150. 热带雨林
151. 溶洞	152. 潮汐	153. 火山	154. 丹霞地貌	155. 冰山/冰川/雪山
156. 海市蜃楼	157. 沙漠	158. 隧道	159. 山脊/山坡	160. 林荫大道
161. 赤道	162. 海洋公园	163. 游乐场	164. 动物园	165. 植物园
166. 台湾海峡/英吉利海峡	167. 海岸/海滩/沙滩	168. 塔/阁/亭/厅/廊/室/台/楼	169. 牛津/剑桥	170. 哈佛/耶鲁
171. 大学/学院/研究所	172. 研究院/音乐学院	173. 学部/系/研究生院	174. 斯坦福/麻省理工	175. 海德堡/哥廷根/莱比锡
176. 悉尼歌剧院	177. 埃菲尔铁塔	178. 阿尔卑斯山	179. 尼亚加拉瀑布	180. 巴黎圣母院
181. 二条城	182. 大王宫	183. 白金汉宫	184. 斗兽场	185. 维也纳金色大厅
186. 美人鱼像	187. 卢浮宫	188. 凯旋门	189. 枫丹白露	190. 埃及金字塔

世界地图

请参见正式出版的世界地图,此处省略。

Group Project

Please translate the following tour guide speech of welcome by the local guide into Chinese.
Hello everybody,

I hope you can all hear me.

My name is Mary. I am one of the three local guides that will accompany you on a conducted walk round the city tomorrow morning. The other guides are Peter and Tracy.

The tour starts at 10 o'clock sharp and lasts about two hours. We will assemble outside the hotel entrance. We will split up into three groups to make it easier for you to hear what is being said.

Unless you are wearing a waterproof anorak, I suggest you bring a raincoat or umbrella as the forecast is not too promising. And wear stout walking shoes if you can.

Don't forget your camera as there will be lots of opportunities to take pictures.

We will have a look at the cathedral, walk through the botanical gardens, and visit the fruit and vegetable market. The tour takes us past the war memorial and along the river.

The tour will end at the Shakespeare tea-room in the main square where you will be able to enjoy a slice of our famous Dundee cake.

Tracy is the history expert. So, if any of you are interested in historical details I suggest that you ask to join her group so that you can pick her brains.

A word of advice. There are morning services in the cathedral, so please be especially quiet when we are there so as not to disturb the worshippers.

If anyone would like a plan of the city showing the route we will be following, I will be happy to give you one afterwards.

If you are interested to read more about our fascinating city and all its wonderful buildings and ancient monuments, there is an illustrated guide on sale at the reception desk. It costs £2.50.

I hope you will enjoy the tour. See you in the morning, 10 o'clock sharp. Try not to be late!

Assignment 1 Role-play Tasks

Scenario 1 - A

Please prepare a role-play based on the following scenario with your group members according to the practical guiding procedure.

中旅总社通知：导游李晨 (Role 1) 接机，引导 23 人美国团住昆仑饭店。

Group Ref. No.: CW-20-09-07

Tour Escort：Richard Steward (Role 2) from: Billy Travel Mississippi

Unexpected cases that Li Chen encountered in the welcoming procedure:

Tourist A: Lois Thompson 行李晚到 (Role 3)

Luggage Claim Receptionist：刘佳 (Intern) (Role 4)

Tourist B: Jason Kimberley 上厕所掉队 (Role 5)

Tourist C: Kim-sung Wong 着急换人民币 (Role 6)

Tourist D: Tony Swain 着急买电话卡 (Role 7)

Tourist E: Ms. Janet Asher 拍照掉队 (Role 8)

Unit 2

Scenario Warm-up 2 Accomodation

Culture Interpretation 2 Hotel Culture

Assignment 2 Role-play Tasks

Scenario Warm-up 2 Accommodation

Listening Extract 2

Two guests check in at the reception of the Cape Grace Hotel in Cape Town, South Africa. Listen and put the following actions in the correct order. Is the receptionist polite?

(   ) a) Requests the guests' passports

(   ) b) Informs the guests of the check-out time

(   ) c) Asks the guests their names

(   ) d) Greets the guests

(   ) e) Advises them about the time for breakfast

(   ) f) Checks how to spell their surname

(   ) g) Gives the room number and directions

(   ) h) Offers to have a porter carry their luggage

Listening Transcript for Extract 2

(Courtesy of Dubicka & O'Keeffe, English for International Tourism Pre-intermediate Students' Book, Unit 7, Exercise 2: 135–136)

Beverley	Good morning. How can I help you?
Robert	Hi, we've booked a room.
Beverley	Could I have the name, please?
Robert	Sure, it's Mr. and Mrs. Robert O'Donnell.
Beverley	Could you spell your surname for me, sir?
Robert	O-apostrophe-D-O-N-N-E-L-L.
Beverley	Thank you, I'll just check on our computer. Yes, Mr. O'Donnell, a double room for three nights. Would you mind showing me your passports, please?
Robert	Our passports? Why do you need them?
Beverley	It's usual practice in South Africa, sir, to record the passport numbers of guests.
Robert	Then I guess so. Leeta Honey, where are the passports?
Leeta	Here Bob, I have them in my bag.
Beverley	Thank you. Would you like me to call your room when the passports are ready for collection?
Robert	What? You want to keep them!
Beverley	It's just to save time now, sir. I can type the details into the computer later. Or do you mind waiting here now?
Robert	Yes, I certainly do. We're tired after that flight and I need a shower and a rest.
Beverley	I understand, sir. Here's your key. You're in room two sixteen. Take the lift to the second floor and turn right. Would you like the porter to help you with your luggage?
Leeta	Yes, please. Now Bob, don't lift anything with your bad back.
Beverley	I'll call the porter for you. Breakfast is served from 8:00 a.m. until 9:30

a.m. Check-out time is at twelve noon on the day of departure. Enjoy your stay and let us know if you need anything.

Leeta   Thank you, miss.

Robert   But Leeta, I don't see why I can't carry the bags...

Listening Extract 3

3.1 A woman reserves a hotel room over the phone. In what order would you expect these questions to be asked? Listen and check your answers.

( ) a) How will you be paying?
( ) b) How many people would that be for?
( ) c) When would that be for exactly?
( ) d) What time will you be arriving?
( ) e) What kind of room would you like?
( ) f) Could I have your name?
( ) g) How many nights will you be staying?

3. 2 Look at the reservation screen below. Then listen again and complete Ann Herridge's booking.

Booking: from 1	Nights 2
Guest: Surname 3	First name 4
Adults 5	Children 6
Address 7	
Room Type: SGL / DBL / TWB / SUITE 8	
Smoking / Non-smoking 9	
Number: 10	
Rate: 11	
Extras: 12	
Return guest: Yes / No 13	
Previous room No.: 14	
Payment: VISA / DEBIT / CHEQUE / CASH 15	
Credit card No.: 16	

23

Listening Transcript for Extract 3

(Courtesy of Strutt, English for International Tourism Intermediate Students' Book, Unit 7, Exercise 2: 134–135)

Receptionist	King James Hotel. How can I help you?
Caller	Hello, I'd like to book a room for my husband and myself, please.
Receptionist	Hold the line, please. I'll put you through to Reservations.
Reservationist	Reservations.
Caller	Good afternoon, I'd like to make a booking for myself and my husband.
Reservationist	Could I have your name, please?
Caller	Yes, it's Herridge — Ann Herridge. H-E-R-R-I-D-G-E.
Reservationist	OK. And when would you like to come?
Caller	The weekend of the 15 July — for two days, please.
Reservationist	I'm sorry Mrs. Herridge, will that be one or two nights?
Caller	Oh, yes. Sorry, two days and two nights — arriving on the 15th and leaving on the 17th.
Reservationist	And that would be a double room, would it? Would you prefer smoking or non-smoking?
Caller	Non-smoking, please. Oh, and the last time we came, we stayed in a room at the back of the hotel overlooking the park. Do you know if we could have the same room? I think it was Room 103.
Reservationist	Hold the line, please. I'll just check. I'm afraid we don't have exactly the same room but I can put you in 205 — it's got the same view and a balcony. The rate's slightly more expensive — £110 per person.
Caller	Well, that's all right, we'll take that.
Reservationist	Fine. How will you be paying, Mrs. Herridge?
Caller	By credit card, Visa.
Reservationist	Could you give me the number, please?

Caller	Yes, it's 4999 1825 6857 6238.
Reservationist	So that's 4999 1825 6857 6238 and your address, please?
Caller	25, Oldham Road, Manchester.
Reservationist	O-L-D-H-A-M?
Caller	That's right. In Manchester.
Reservationist	Right, Mrs. Herridge, I've made the reservation. We look forward to seeing you again on the 15th.
Caller	Thank you.
Reservationist	You're welcome. Goodbye.
Caller	Oh, I nearly forgot, I was wondering if you could arrange for a bottle of champagne to be in the room when we come, it's our wedding anniversary.
Reservationist	That's no problem. I've made a note and it'll be ready when you arrive.
Caller	Thank you so much. Goodbye.
Reservationist	Goodbye.

Listening Extract 4

Look at the registration card below. Then listen to a conversation at the reception desk and complete the card.

King James Hotel

The undersigned authorizes the King James Hotel to use data collected in this questionnaire for sales and marketing purposes.

Arrival _____ 1	Type _____ 5
Departure _____ 2	Surname _____ 6
Room No. _____ 3	Nationality _____ 7
Rate _____ 4	Passport No. _____ 8

Method of payment 9 (please tick as appropriate)

☐ Cash £   ☐ Credit Card £   ☐ Travel Voucher £   ☐ Charge to Company £

Listening Transcript for Extract 4

(Courtesy of Strutt, English for International Tourism Intermediate Students' Book, Unit 7, Exercise 4: 135)

Receptionis	Good afternoon.
Guest	Good afternoon. We'd like to book a room, please.
Receptionist	Fine, what kind of room would you like?
Guest	A single room with bath, please. Oh, and a king-sized bed.
Receptionist	I'll just check that we have a room free. Yes, that's OK. Could you tell me your name?
Guest	Yes, it's Jan Urbanik. That's J-A-N and the surname is U-R-B-A-N-I-K.
Receptionist	OK, I've got that. And your nationality?
Guest	Polish.
Receptionist	And how long will you be staying?
Guest	Just a couple of nights, until 8th December.
Receptionist	So that's a double room for two nights.
Guest	Yes, can you tell me the price?
Receptionist	Yes, it's £95 per night, breakfast included. And could I just take your passport number?
Guest	Yes, I have it here... It's EG6662781.
Receptionist	Fine, and how will you be paying, Mr. Urbanik?
Guest	With a Visa Card.
Receptionist	OK, if I can just take an imprint of the card. Thank you. Right, well here's your key and your room number is 19, on the first floor.
Guest	Thank you.

Listening Extract 5

Listen to Mr. Collins checking out of the Admiral Hotel in St. Petersburg. How does he react to the bill? Why?

1. What did Mr. Collins order from room service?
   _____

2. Where is the information about prices?
   _____

3. Who did Mr. Collins telephone?
   _____

4. Why are the phone calls from the hotel expensive?
   _____

5. What is the correct total amount for the bill?
   _____

6. How is he going to pay the bill?
   _____

Look at the Hotel Bill. What extra costs are usually added to a hotel bill?

The Admiral Hotel

Bed and buffet breakfast 3 nights @ 417	7,950
Room Service	235
Minibar	47
Telephone calls	1,740
Registration fee	87
Tax (7%)	704
Total	RUB10,763

5% sales tax when paying by credit card.
Thank you for choosing The Admiral Hotel. We hope you enjoyed your stay.

Listening Transcript for Extract 5

(Courtesy of Dubicka & O'Keeffe, English for International Tourism Pre-intermediate Students' Book, Unit 14, Exercise 2: 142)

Receptionist Are you checking out now, sir?

Collins Yes, that's right. Room four one seven.

Recptionist Here's your bill, Mr. Collins. How would you like to pay?

Collins Hold on a minute, this can't be right. It says here 10,763 roubles. I think there's been a mistake. I've been overcharged.

Receptionist I'll just check that for you. The total includes room service which you ordered on the evening of the eighteenth. It was a chicken sandwich and a pot of coffee.

Collins Yes, that's right.

Receptionist This amount here is for the drinks you had from the minibar in your room.

Collins Yes, yes, but what's this 704 roubles for?

Receptionist That's the local government tax, which we have to charge. It's explained in the hotel information pack in your room.

Collins Well, what about this amount for phone calls? I don't remember making any phone calls.

Receptionist I'll just check our records. It says here that there was a call to the United Kingdom yesterday evening.

Collins Oh, yes, that's right — I called my wife. But I was only on the phone for a couple of minutes — I can't believe it cost that much.

Receptionist We do have our own satellite dish here at the hotel, which adds to the cost. But I'll just check that for you. Oh, yes, I do apologize, we have made a mistake here. This isn't the right amount, it should be 1,760 roubles, not 1,740. That makes a total of 10,783 roubles.

Collins But you can't charge me even more for that phone call!

Receptionist I'm sorry, sir. Would you like to pay by cash or credit card? I have to point out that there is a five percent surcharge if you want to pay by credit card.

Collins Oh, no, it's already expensive enough. I'll pay by cash.

Listening Extract 6

A guest checking in at a hotel loses something of value. Read the following list of events. Then listen and number the events in the order in which they occur.

(   ) a) The porter shows Mrs. Horton to Room 212.
(   ) b) Mrs. Horton reports the missing necklace to reception.
(   ) c) Mrs. Horton goes to her room.
(   ) d) Mrs. Horton telephones her husband.
(   ) e) Mrs. Horton unpacks her clothes and uses the bathroom.
(   ) f) The receptionist offers to ring the housekeeper.
(   ) g) The receptionist misunderstands the name.

Listening Transcript for Extract 6

(Courtesy of Strutt, English for International Tourism Intermediate Students' Book, Unit 5, Exercise 15: 133)

Part One

Receptionist A	Good morning, can I help you?
Mrs. Horton	Yes, my name's Mrs. Horton and I've a reservation for myself and my husband.
Receptionist A	Fine. Yes. Sorry, can you give me your name again?
Mrs. Horton	Yes, Horton. I phoned yesterday.
Receptionist A	Orton. Sorry I can't see your name.
Mrs. Horton	Horton, H-O-R-T-O-N.
Receptionist A	Ah, yes, very sorry. The porter will take you to your room, 112. Is that your luggage?
Mrs. Horton	Yes.
Receptionist A	OK, well, if you come this way, please.

Part Two

Mrs. Horton	Hello, I've just been given a room, Room 112 I think it is, but I'm afraid it's really very unsuitable. It's extremely small and I can hear the people in the next room. I really feel that with the prices you're charging the rooms should be much better than this one.
Receptionist A	Ah, I'm sorry to hear that, can you give me the room number?
Mrs. Horton	112.
Receptionist A	Right, Mrs. Horton, I'll ask the porter to show you another room and if you find it suitable we can move you.
Mrs. Horton	I'll wait for him to arrive.
Receptionist A	Right, thank you.

Unit 2

Part Three

Receptionist A	Ah, Joe, did you show Mrs. Horton the room?
Porter	Yes, she's gone into 212 but I don't know whether it was a good idea — she'd unpacked half her stuff, there were clothes all over the place and she'd already used the bathroom.
Receptionist A	Oh, dear, did you help her move?
Porter	Yes, but she's going to be a difficult guest.
Receptionist A	OK. Well, thanks anyway.

Part Four

Mrs. Horton	Hello, this is Mrs. Horton in Room 212.
Receptionist B	Ah, hello, Mrs. Horton. Is the room to your satisfaction?
Mrs. Horton	I'm not bothered about the room. My diamond necklace is missing. I had it in my suitcase with my blue dress and I can't find it anywhere.
Receptionist B	Oh, dear, you say it was in your suitcase?
Mrs. Horton	Yes. But I took it out and I'm sure I put it on the bed.
Receptionist B	Well, it must still be in the room you had before. I'll ring the housekeeper and have the room searched for you. I'm sure it'll turn up.
Mrs. Horton	I've had it for 25 years and it's worth a lot of money. I can't understand what's happened to it. My husband is going to hear about this!

Part Five

House Keeper	I can't find it anywhere. I've looked everywhere in both rooms and it's nowhere to be found.
Receptionist B	Oh, dear, so what is she doing now?
House Keeper	She's phoned her husband who apparently is in a meeting at the moment. She's taken a sleeping pill.
Receptionist B	OK. Well tell me if anything happens.

Listening Extract 7

Later that afternoon, Mr. Horton arrives at reception. Listen and answer these questions.

1. What does he think has happened to the necklace?
   _____

2. What does Mr. Horton want to know?
   _____

3. What explanation does the receptionist give him?
   _____

4. Why can't Mr. Horton find his wife?
   _____

5. Why couldn't Mr. Horton speak to his wife on the phone?
   _____

Send a memo to the Duty Manager to tell her what has happened and what action has been taken.

Memo

TO: DATE:

FROM: CC:

SUBJECT:

Listening Transcript for Extract 7

(Courtesy of Strutt, English for International Tourism Intermediate Students' Book, Unit 5, Exercise 17: 133–134)

Receptionist A	Good afternoon. Can I help you?
Mr. Horton	I hope so. It's absolutely scandalous.
Receptionist A	What seems to be the problem, sir?
Mr. Horton	I'll tell you what the problem is. My wife, Mrs. Horton in Room 112, checked in here and was given a tiny room. She unpacked and then she was moved into another room. Meanwhile, her diamond necklace was either lost or maybe stolen. At work I was interrupted with a message during an important meeting. I phoned the hotel and got through to a total stranger in another room. I've just been up to my room and it's locked and I don't know where my wife is.
Receptionist A	Sorry, I think there's been some sort of misunderstanding. You're Mr. Horton, is that right?
Mr. Horton	Yes.
Receptionist A	Well, if I could just explain the situation. When your wife arrived she was unhappy with her room so we helped her move into a more comfortable one. She then said she had mislaid her necklace and I had the room searched by the housekeeper. Unfortunately, we haven't been able to find the necklace yet and your wife, as I understand it, is resting in her room.
Mr. Horton	Oh. Well, why isn't she in her room now? It's locked and there's no answer.
Receptionist A	Well, as I said, she's now in another room, Room 212.
Mr. Horton	And why wasn't I able to speak to her when I phoned?
Receptionist A	I think I can explain that. What seems to have happened is that the switchboard did not know that your room had been

	changed so they put you through to 112 instead of 212.
Mr. Horton	That's incredibly inefficient!
Receptionist A	I apologize for the inconvenience Mr. Horton. But I think the main thing now is to try to sort out the problem of the missing necklace. What I suggest we do if the necklace cannot be found is that we...

Culture Interpretation 2 Hotel Culture

Vocabulary Workshop

Below are hotel-industry related words. Please translate them into English with your partners.

1. 预订	2. 登记/登记簿	3. 入住手续	4. 退房手续	5. 前台
6. 收银	7. 行李车	8. 礼宾部	9. 问询处	10. 货币兑换
11. 失物招领	12. 贵重物品	13. 寄存/押金	14. 投诉	15. 房费
16. 退款/扣除	17. 衣帽间	18. 房价表	19. 打折	20. 宣传册
21. 信用卡	22. 现金	23. 旅行支票	24. 报销	25. 饭店名片
26. 酒吧	27. 自助餐	28. 现点	29. 套餐	30. 宴会
31. 食堂	32. 餐厅/餐馆	33. 便利店	34. 送餐服务	35. 精品廊
36. 双人标间	37. 单人间	38. 婴儿床	39. 套间	40. 大床房
41. 贵宾室/会议室	42. 记者会	43. 分机/长途/国际长途	44. 传真/电话亭	45. 太平门/紧急出口
46. 商务中心	47. 上网接口	48. 打印/复印	49. 门禁电话	50. 信封/包裹

51. 前台服务员	52. 客房服务员	53. 餐厅服务员	54. 值班经理	55. 门童/行李员
56. 房卡/餐券	57. 发票/收据	58. 手纸	59. 男/女厕所	60. 厕所/马桶
61. 台盆/龙头	62. 干手器	63. 镜子/梳子	64. 拖鞋/鞋擦	65. 熨斗/衣架
66. 转换插头	67. 吹风机	68. 剃须刀/膏	69. 万用插座	70. 遥控器
71. 洗手液	72. 洗衣袋	73. 花洒/浴缸	74. 香皂/香水	75. 纸巾/湿巾
76. 洗面奶	77. 洗发水	78. 护发素	79. 沐浴液	80. 润肤露
81. 浴巾/浴帽	82. 唇膏	83. 棉签	84. 针线包	85. 牙刷/牙膏
86. 被子	87. 床罩	88. 床单	89. 毯子	90. 床垫
91. 地毯	92. 靠垫/坐垫	93. 枕头	94. 空调	95. 冰箱/冰柜
96. 饮水机	97. 电水壶	98. 电视	99. 台式电脑	100. 手提电脑
101. 开关	102. 台灯	103. 断电/充电	104. 维修	105. 客房酒柜
106. 租借	107. 婴儿车	108. 轮椅	109. 雨伞/拐杖	110. 大堂
111. 送餐车	112. 投影仪	113. 大屏幕	114. 扩音器	115. 麦克风
116. 叫早服务	117. 票务中心	118. 按摩	119. 医务室	120. 康乐中心
121. 急救	122. 男女发廊	123. 电梯	124. 扶梯/直梯	125. 柜台

Group Project: Hotel Service Class Drama

Scene 1: Room Reservation

You work at the reservation desk, Kunlun Hotel. Please role-play with your group based on the scenarios given below. Creative improvisations are encouraged. The following worksheet could be used as a reference.

A. Miss Elisabeth O'Dell telephones to book a 3-night-stay with her friend Miss Maggie Frierson. Then she phones again for adding one more bed for her another friend Natalie Horridge. They are all non-smokers and vegetarians. They need room service.	B. Mrs. Susanna Hembry wants to book a 4-day-stay for her whole family (her 2 daughters — 12/10 years old and 1 son — 6 years old, her mother and father, her sister and brother-in-law). Please help her to decide the suitable room types and help to complete the booking.
C. Mr. Henry Kings telephones to book a 2-night-stay with his bride for their honeymoon travel. His wife has slight insomnia so he wants a quiet room. He also wants a room with internet connection point. They will pay by debit card because their credit card is going to expire. They need only one breakfast.	D. Ms. Linda Scruton wants to book a suite room for her uncle Edward Scruton who needs to take a business trip in Beijing for one week. She stayed in Kunlun Hotel 3 years ago and she asks if it is possible to provide the same type of room and the same service for her uncle.

Hotel Reservation Form

Booking from	Nights:
Guest Surname:	First name:
Citizen ID/Passport No.:	Tel.:
Adults:	Children:
Address:	
Room Type: SGL / DBL / TWB / SUITE	
Smoking/Non-smoking	
Number:	
Rate:	
Extras:	
Return guest: Yes / No	
Previous room No.:	
Payment: CREDIT CARD/DEBIT CARD/CHEQUE/CASH	
Credit card No.:	

Scene 2: Concierge

You are on duty at concierge this evening when your colleague working at the airport representative desk escorts a lady guest named Malvina fumbling her way into the hotel lobby because she just lost her contact lenses at the airport toilet. Your colleague tells you this lady has just checked in and she/he must leave now and you are asked to guarantee her smooth stay at your hotel. However, the lady first asks you if you could help to rent a taxi because she wants to go to the optician store to buy new contact lenses. Then you tell her it is too late to go to the optician now and arrange one bell-boy to help her with her luggage and help her familiarize the hotel facilities such as the location of the lift, lobby settings, and how to go to the restaurant to take her breakfast tomorrow morning, etc. Then you ask her floor housekeeper to help her familiarize the room settings like the use of the key, the light switch, the air conditioner switch, the bathroom facilities, the table stand control panels, the TV controller, the beddings, the electric pot, the free tea, the mini-bar, the room service menu, the telephone directory, the clothes racks, etc. and do the turndown service for her.

Scene 3: Check-in

It is 8:40 p.m. Wang Jia and Faulkner guide a group of 20 tired tourists (4 male single, 9 female single, 1 couple with 3 kids, 1 couple) to the hotel lobby. They come to the reception to check-in for 2 triple rooms, 5 twin rooms, 2 double rooms, 1 single room for 3 nights they reserved one month ago. However, they are told 2 of the twin rooms they booked have been given to other groups because they did not check in before 8:00 p.m. and only triple rooms and suite double rooms available can be provided for them. Just at that time, a member of the group, Julia, comes to Faulkner to complain about her roommate and asks if it is possible to help to change a room for her. Please role-play it with your group based on the following cue card.

Receptionist	Wang Jia
1. Ask for proof and details of the booking. 2. Show sympathy to the group. 3. Explain the hotel's booking rule to them. 4. Help the group to upgrade the booking.	1. Confirm the booking details. 2. Explain because the flight was delayed and ask for upgrading. 3. Arrange morning call. 4. Give instructions to the group on hotel facilities. 5. Declare assembly time and place.
Faulkner	**Julia**
1. Show the confirming fax copy to the reception. 2. Complain about overbooking and ask for compensation. 3. Re-allocate the rooms. 4. Collect passports. 5. Assign keys to the tourists.	1. Can't sleep well due to her roommate's snoring. 2. Ask for changing a room even by affording more room charge because her roommate is a smoker.

Scene 4: Check-out

A group of guests Mr. & Mrs. White (Eric & Helen) and their daughter Malvina with two kids (Grace & Maggie) queue to check-out at the reception desk. They can't understand why they are charged such a lot. Receptionist Miss Wu Qiong is on duty then, and she tries to explain the bill to them. When they are to leave, Maggie tells Malvina she might leave her doll in the room. However, housekeeper Sun Hong telephones there is nothing left in Malvina's room but a cane left in the old couple's room. Then what happens next? Please role-play with your group members based on the scenarios and worksheet given below.

Rail Hotel

Queen bed and buffet breakfast 3 nights @ 2,650	RMB1,950
Room service	RMB235
Minibar	RMB47
Telephone calls	RMB740
Laundry service	RMB187
Hotel bar drinks	RMB704
Total	**RMB3,863**

Thank you for choosing Rail Hotel. We hope you enjoyed your stay.

===

Rail Hotel

King bed and buffet breakfast 3 nights @ 2,687	RMB2,250
Extra bed charge	RMB450
Room service	RMB498
Minibar	RMB669
Telephone calls	RMB1,257
Laundry service	RMB439
Hotel bar drinks	RMB2,304
Total	**RMB7,867**

Thank you for choosing Rail Hotel. We hope you enjoyed your stay.

Scene 5: Reception

5.1 Ms. Maria Leech is a private assistant of Madame Catherine Steward—a famous fashion designer. These two ladies stay in Room 3567 and Room 3478 (suite room) at your hotel respectively. This morning, before they go out, Maria comes to ask the receptionist (Miss Wang Jia) to transfer a folder containing Madame Steward's new design pictures to her friend Mr. Nick Patterson around 3 o'clock this afternoon, and offers the photo of Nick to Wang as a reference. She reminds her of never passing the folder to the wrong person as some small fashion magazine journalists may be interested in exposing the design information in advance. In the afternoon, Wang Jia is duty off and it is her colleague Li Tao who will receive Nick. However, before Nick comes to your hotel, a fashion journalist resembling him arrives first, then what happens next? Please role-play the story based on the forgoing scenario with your group members.

5.2 Two amateur photographers with a local map come to the reception to enquire about the places where the local people's happy life can be fully reflected. The aspects they are interested in are the schools, the neighborhood's activities, the shopping people, as well as the people at the entertainment or catering sites. Please recommend some places to them and tell them how to go there. And then they ask if it is possible to deposit their big cameras, camcorders, laptops, etc. at the reception since they will attend a dinner party in Tianjin early the next morning and probably come back in the late evening. Li Tao helps to go through the deposit procedure and arrangs bellboy Song Jian to take out the equipment. Then they ask where they could buy SD cards as theirs are full. Then Song Jian is asked to guide them to the hotel shop.

Message Worksheet for Scene 5

Kunlun Hotel

==

Guest Name: _____ Room No.: _____

==

To Mr./Ms./Miss _____ Date: _____ (DD/MM/YY)

Please call back at: _____ (TEL)

Scene 6: Housekeeping & Operator

6.1 Wang Yue is on duty at the Housekeeper Hotline. This morning she receives a complaint phone call from Room 2409. It is Mrs. Janet Asher with chronic rheumatism checking in yesterday. She stays with her daughter together. She tells Wang that she couldn't find the wool blanket last night, so she had to use her overcoat together with the bed cover to keep warm for her and her 10 year-old-daughter Laura . She phones to complain that both she and her daughter may catch heavy cold because of their running noses, coughs and sneezes apart from her pain on her knees. She strongly asks to bring thick duvet to her. Wang soon arranges a housekeeper — Liu Xiao-dan to send a quilt and two cups of ginger black tea to her room. Liu unwraps the inner bed sheet and the wool blanket is revealed. Laura feels very embarrassed about that. Xiao Liu also explains to Laura why ginger is added to their tea. Then Janet asks Xiao Liu to help switch the shower into bath which made them very inconvenient since yesterday...

6.2 Lisa Lau, a friend of Janet Asher staying in room 2409 at your hotel, phones from HongKong to leave a message to Janet through concierge clerk Li Nan for buying 2 stuffed pandas for her daughter Nancy. The money will be returned to her when they are back to Hong Kong. When Mrs. Asher comes back to her room, she receives the message forwarded from concierge and then she goes to the concierge desk to enquire some shopping information including where to buy the stuffed pandas in detail, because she also wants to buy some gifts for her family. Please recommend some shopping malls, streets, supermarkets to her and show her how to go there. Then Asher goes to her room and phones the operator to help make a person-to-person call to Lisa in Hong Kong to confirm her request.

Message Worksheet for Scene 6

Kunlun Hotel
==
Guest Name: _____ Room No.: _____
==
To Mr./Ms./Miss _____ Date: _____ (DD/MM/YY)
Please call back at: _____ (TEL)

Scene 7: Restaurant & Room Service

7.1 Suppose Zhao Ying is a receptionist at a famous restaurant specializing in Beijing local flavor. This morning, tour guide Anne Wang calls to reserve a table for 4 in the name of Jenny Smith at your restaurant for tomorrow late evening because they may just come back from the Great Wall then. She tells you there are a vegetarian, one person with diabetes, and one person allergic to alcohol among them. Please take down notes and confirm booking with her.

7.2 At 8:00 p.m. that evening, Jenny comes to your restaurant with her group. However they have big difficulty in reading the Chinese menu because all the dishes' names are written either in Pinyin or in Chinese characters and the trainee waiter/waitress Xiao Liu has strong local accent. Wu Dan, the head waiter, comes to help Xiao Liu to complete the ordering procedure by negotiating with Jenny. The order should involve appetizers or cold dishes, main courses, staple food, desserts, beverages and drinks.

7.3 When Jenny settles the bill, waitress Chen Tao comes to her to explain the items on her bill. Then she goes to the counter to pay by her credit card. Afterwards, a reservation call comes from George Black for room service in room 4509 half an hour later. But he has no idea about what to order and the receptionist on-duty Li Yan recommends a set menu snack food to him and helps send it to his room.

Table Reservation/Room Service Worksheet

Date & Time	Number of Persons	Booked by	Table/Room No.	Requirements

Scene 8: Business Center

8.1 Tony/Elizabeth Gould is a guest of your hotel staying in Room 1409. This morning, he/she calls to the concierge for help when Li Jing is on duty. Tony/Elizabeth asks if they can help him/her to photocopy some documents and send a fax to his/her company's headquarter in Helsinki Finland. Li Jing tells him/her that he/she can do these in the hotel business center which can be found at the second floor beside the hotel café.

8.2 Then Mr./Madame Gould asks his/her secretary Susan/Mark Brown to the business center to fulfil the faxing and copying tasks. What he/she needs to do is to make 5 copies of a 25-page document from a file. Apart from that, the secretary also needs to send a fax to the company head office bearing Gould's signature (fax no.: 0049-2287-4315). Then the secretary brings a file folder to the business center where Liu Chang is on duty. Liu presents a service charge tariff to the secretary and asks him/her to fill in a form which is for the bill settlement.

\multicolumn{5}{c}{**Rail Hotel Business Center Tariff**}				
Guest Name:		Date: (DD/MM/YY)		Room No.:
Photocopy	Paper Size A4	Number of Pages	Paper Size B5	Number of Pages
	1.0 Yuan/Page (Black & White) 10.00 Yuan/Page (Colored)		0.5 Yuan/Page (Black & White) 8.00 Yuan/Page (Colored)	
Fax No.:				
Total Sum:	RMB			Yuan
Way of Payment: ☐Signing Bill ☐Cash ☐Check ☐Credit Card ☐Debit Card ☐Traveler's Check				

8.3 Maria/Johnson Woods is a guest of your hotel staying in Room 1569. This morning she/he comes to the concierge with a large box when Zhou Ying is on duty. Maria/Johnson Woods tells Zhou she/he would like to post a pair of Cloisonné vases to her/his home in Hawaii, U. S. A. Zhou tells Maria/Johnson Woods this department can help send letter mails only and for other postal service the guest needs to go the post office outside the hotel herself/himself. Then Zhou offers Maria/Johnson Woods a guide map and indicates to Maria/Johnson Woods how to walk to the post office from the hotel lobby.

8.4 Chen Huan phones Mr./Mrs. Watson staying in room 2451 and tells him/her that the two tickets for the acrobatic show tomorrow evening at the Sky Bridge Theater have been sent to their department and if it's convenient to send them to their room now. Watson agrees to wait for the bellboy in the room. Then Ms. Helena Wong phones the concierge to ask Chen to help book three air tickets to Nanjing next Wednesday. Chen confirms the booking information with the booking form... Then bellboy Zhou Yongxiang takes the show tickets to the Watsons' room to help confirm the ticket information with them: first floor, row 10, seats 9 & 11; showing time: tomorrow 7:00 — 9:00 p.m.; no smoking & no photographs. The hotel bus will wait for them at the lobby gate and start off at 6:15 p.m..

Rail Hotel Ticket Booking Form

Guest Name:	Booking Date: (DD/MM/YY)		Room Number:
Ticket Title:	Price:	Number:	Date:
Discount:	Total Sum:		
Way of Payment: ☐Signing Bill ☐Cash ☐Check ☐Credit Card ☐Debit Card ☐Traveler's Check			

Scene 9: Health & Recreation

9.1 Helen & Greg Pearson with their family are staying at your hotel. One day, they come to inquire about the health and recreation facilities at your hotel. Their requirements are as follows:

(1) Wife — Helen wants to go to the hair dresser.
(2) Daughter — Alice would like to take sauna bath.
(3) Son — Peter wants to do muscle build-up exercise.
(4) Husband — Greg prefers swimming.

The hotel health center receptionist Wang Zheng first introduces the hotel health facilities to them and then gives some suggestions in terms of their requirements, and finally shows the way to them respectively.

9.2 Anthony/Grace Mayer is a secretary of Grandview Travel Co., Ltd. This afternoon, he/she phones to your hotel health center to book a 2-hour bowling for four VIP clients of his/her company. The clients will come to the center at 3 o'clock. However, receptionist Cui Hao tells him/her this bowling center will only open to the resident guests. After a while, Linda and Michael Williams come to play badminton with their room card. Cui Hao tells them there is no vacancy at present and it needs to be reserved in advance. Then they decide to book 2 hours for tomorrow afternoon. Finally Cui helps them to fill in the booking form.

Rail Hotel Health Center Booking Form

Guest Name:	Room Number:	Date of Booking: (DD/MM/YY)	
Facilities: Tennis□ Badminton□ Bowling□ Sauna-bath□ Swimming Pool□ Gym□			
Time: _____ a.m./p.m. — _____ a.m./p.m. Date: (DD/MM/YY) ___/___/___		Charge: 100 yuan/hour	Total Sum:
Way of Payment: □Signing Bill □Cash □Check □Credit Card □Debit Card □Traveler's Check			

Scene 10: Convention & Miscellaneous Service

10.1 Wang Yang calls to the convention center to book convention service for the company's annual conference. Two rooms are needed altogether: one conference room for all the 159 employees of the company and one VIP sitting room for 16 senior managerial meeting. The conference agenda is as follows:

Date & Time	Event	Venue Needed
20/06/08 9:00—11:30 a.m.	Senior managerial meeting	16-people meeting room
20/06/08 12:00—1:30 p.m.	Buffet lunch	16-people buffet
20/06/08 2:00—5:00 p.m.	Conference for all employees	159-people conference hall
20/12/08 7:00—9:00 p.m.	Dinner party	488-people banquet hall

Rail Hotel Convention Service Booking Form

Guest Name:	Date of Booking: (DD/MM/YY)
Room Type	Room Charge
VIP sitting room (20 people)	100 Yuan/30 minutes
VIP meeting room (20 people)	80 Yuan/30 minutes
Conference press room (120 people)	200 Yuan/30 minutes
Conference Hall (250 people)	350 Yuan/30 minutes

Notes: for food or beverage service please refer to the hotel room service charge.

Total Sum:
Room: _____ Time: _____ a.m./p.m. — _____ a.m./p.m.
Room: _____ Time: _____ a.m./p.m. — _____ a.m./p.m.

Way of Payment:
☐Signing Bill ☐Cash ☐Check ☐Credit Card ☐Debit Card ☐Traveler's Check

10.2 Mr. and Mrs. Black from room 2307 would like to go to see a friend in this city but their twin daughters wouldn't like to go with them. So they have to send their daughters to the hotel concierge to help attend them (maybe 3 hours) this evening. The receptionist Wu Ying tells them they will be charged 50 yuan per child per hour for baby-sitting. When the Blacks would like to pay in US dollars, they are told to go to the foreign currency exchange counter first because this hotel won't accept US dollars but RMB only.

Role-play Tutorial

Before you design your plot, please decide how many roles should be involved in the play and use the following worksheet to assign these roles to each member of your group.

Role Assignment Worksheet

Name	Role
1	
2	
3	
4	
5	
6	
7	
8	
Director:	Date:

Assignment 2 Role-play Tasks

Role 1 Receptionist
Role 2 Tour Escort: Miss Emma Faulkner/Mr. Grover Faulkner
Role 3 National Guide: 王佳 (Jenny/Jack)
Role 4 Guest A: Mr. Eric Haggit (70 years old gentleman with poor memory)
Role 5 Guest B: Miss. Julia Shears (45 years old lady with light insomnia, allergic to smoke)
Role 6 Guest C: Mrs. Malvina O'Foody (37 years old lady, traveling with her husband and 3 kids)

Scenario 2 - A

It is 8:40 p.m. Wang Jia and Faulkner guide a group of 20 tired tourists (4 male single + 9 female single + 1 couple with 3 kids + 1 couple) to the hotel lobby.

They come to the reception to check-in for 2 triple rooms, 5 twin rooms, 2 double rooms, 1 single room for 3 nights they reserved one month ago. However, they are told 2 of the twin rooms they booked have been given to other groups because they did not check in before 8 p.m. and only triple rooms and suite double rooms available can be provided for them. Then what happens?

Please role-play it with your group based on the following cue card.

Receptionist	Wang Jia	Faulkner
1. Ask for proof and details of the booking.	1. Confirm the booking details.	1. Show the confirming fax copy to the reception.
2. Show sympathy to the group.	2. Explain because the flight was delayed and ask for upgrading.	2. Complain about overbooking and ask for compensation.
3. Explain the hotel's booking rule to them.	3. Arrange morning call.	3. Re-allocate the rooms.
4. Help the group to upgrade the booking.	4. Give instructions to the group on hotel facilities.	4. Collect passports.
	5. Declare assembly time and place.	5. Assign keys to the tourists.

Scenario 2 - B

In the late afternoon, when Wang Jia and Faulkner are waiting for the tourists in the hotel lobby, Eric, Julia and Malvina come to make complaints to them respectively. Both Wang and Faulkner try to console them and help to offer feasible solutions for them. Please role-play it based on the following cue card.

Eric	Julia	Malvina
Can't find his umbrella anywhere. It is very important to him because it can be used as walking stick. He thinks he lost his camera in Tokyo—the last leg of their journey but he is also told that it has been seen using in Beijing.	Can't sleep well due to her roommate's snoring. Complain about the lunch and supper because she is a vegetarian. Ask for changing a room even by affording more room charge because her roommate is a smoker.	Originally 1 double room and 1 triple room were allocated to her family, but due to overbooking, her kids are arranged to 1 double room with a king-size bed. She asks for adding one single bed to the kids' room.

Unit 3

Scenario Warm-up 3 Catering

Culture Interpretation 3 Chinese Cuisine

Assignment 3 Role-play Tasks

Unit 3

Scenario Warm-up 3 Catering

Listening Extract 8

8.1 You will hear two people ordering food. Listen and answer these questions.

1. What do they order to drink?

_____

2. Have they been to this restaurant before?

_____

3. What starters do they order?

_____

4. For what reason does Paul choose this starter?

_____

5. What main courses do they order?

_____

6. What special request does Mary make?

_____

7. What is a choron sauce?

_____

8. What are they going to drink with their meal?

_____

8.2 Listen to the waiter taking the order again and complete these phrases.

Step 1 Show the guests to the table

1. *If you would like to* follow me, please?
2. Shall I _____ madam?

Step 2 Present the menu and take the drinks order

3. _____ Menu.
4. Would you like _____ ?

Step 3 Take the order

5. _____ order?
6. _____ to drink?

Step 4 Make any necessary recommendations

7. _____ the Cabernet Sauvigon, madam.

Step 5 Repeat the order to make sure it is correct

8. _____ one soup of the day, one escargots...

Listening Transcript for Extract 8

(Courtesy of Strutt, English for International Tourism Intermediate Students' Book, Unit 10, Exercise 17: 140)

Waiter	Bonsoir, vous avez réservé?
Paul	Non, nous n'avons pas. I'm sorry but we don't speak French.
Waiter	OK, that does not matter. So, there are two of you?
Paul	That's right.
Waiter	If you would like to follow me, please. There's a table free by the window. If you would like to sit down. Shall I take your coat, madam?
Mary	Oh, thank you.
Waiter	And here's the menu. Would you like something to drink before your meal?
Paul	Mary?
Mary	Yes, good idea. What have you got?
Waiter	Martini, Cinzano, Kir — that is white wine with a blackcurrant liqueur, or...
Mary	I'll have a kir.
Paul	Yes, I'll have a kir too.
Waiter	Two kirs.
Mary	Have you been here before?
Paul	Actually, it was John who recommended this particular restaurant to me but I've never been here myself.
Mary	Well, it's certainly very pleasant. I'm not entirely sure but I've a feeling I came here for a working lunch a few years ago. Oh, thank you.
Paul	Thank you.
Waiter	Are you ready to order?
Paul	Mary?
Mary	I think so. But could you tell me what the soup of the day is?
Paul	Certainly. Today we're serving a Gratinée à l'Oignon. That is a French onion soup topped with croutons and cheese.
Mary	Sounds good to me. I'll have that. What do you fancy?

Paul	I think I'll have the snails. After all, we are in France!
Waiter	And to follow?
Mary	OK, I'll have the rack of lamb, please but could you do it without the mint sauce, please? I'm allergic to mint.
Paul	Yeah, the lamb looks good. Could you tell me what a choron sauce is?
Waiter	Ah, yes of course. Er... Choron sauce was created by a man called Alexander Etienne Choron, a famous French chef of the 19th century. Choron sauce is a delicious Béarnaise sauce with a tomato puree.
Paul	OK, I'll have that!
Waiter	And What would you like to drink?
Mary	What would you recommend?
Waiter	I'd certainly recommend the Cabernet Sauvignon, madam.
Paul	So, we'll have a bottle of that, please.
Waiter	Thank you. So that's one soup of the day and one plate of snails followed by two racks of lamb and a bottle of Cabernet Sauvignon.
Paul	That's right.
Waiter	Thank you, sir.

Culture Interpretation 3 Chinese Cuisine

Vocabulary Workshop

What's your favorite food? Please share your ideas with your group members. Do you know how to translate the following expressions into English? You may refer to the word list attached below.

1. 四川泡菜	2. 小葱拌豆腐	3. 北京豆酱	4. 大丰收	5. 冷荤拼盘
6. 宫保鸡丁	7. 黑椒牛柳	8. 糖醋里脊	9. 鱼香肉丝	10. 烤乳猪
11. 清蒸鲥鱼	12. 红烧狮子头	13. 蚝油生菜	14. 番茄炒鸡蛋	15. 香菇油菜
16. 炸酱面	17. 扬州炒饭	18. 鸡丝凉面	19. 肠粉/春卷	20. 星洲米粉
21. 莲藕排骨汤	22. 北京烤鸭	23. 杏仁豆腐	24. 蟹黄豆腐羹	25. 拔丝山药
26. 红豆粥	27. 皮蛋肉粥	28. 绿豆粥	29. 小米粥	30. 汤圆
31. 烧卖（麦）	32. 小笼包	33. 肉夹馍	34. 褡裢火烧	35. 驴肉烧饼
36. 年糕	37. 粽子	38. 煎饼	39. 羊肉串	40. 豆浆
41. 饺子	42. 金银馒头	43. 馄饨	44. 土豆泥	45. 茶汤
46. 烤香肠	47. 爆米花	48. 蛋挞	49. 糖葫芦	50. 麻辣烫
51. 冰棍儿	52. 汽水	53. 凉茶	54. 芝麻糊	55. 鸡蛋羹

Supplementary Vocabulary

烹饪技巧类 Service Type & Cooking Skills	菜品味道或质感类常用词 Taste
自助 buffet	脆 crisp
零点 a la carte	生 raw
套餐 table d'hote	老 tough/overdone
铁板 sizzling	腻 greasy
烘 bake	咸 salty
熏 smoke	甜 sweet
烤 roast/barbecue	酸 sour
炒/煎/炸 fry	苦 bitter
蒸 steam	辣 spicy/hot
炖 simmer/stew	辛辣 pungent
煮 boil	
宫保 kung-pao	

餐具类 Table Ware	
筷子 chopsticks	托盘 tray
刀 knife	筷子托 chopstick rest
叉 fork	餐巾/纸巾 napkin
勺 spoon	牙签 toothtick
漏勺 strainer ladle	菜单 menu
杯子 cup	账单 bill
马克杯（单柄大杯）mug	蒸笼 steamer
玻璃杯 glass	铁板 sizzle platter
碗 bowl	干锅 dry wok/stir fry
碟子 dish	火锅 hotpot
盘子 plate	瑞士火锅 fondue
茶壶 teapot	

调料类 Seasonings & Dressings	
味精 MSG	豆豉 fermented soybean
孜然 cumin	大葱 leek
芥末 mustard	小葱（葱青）scallion
姜 ginger	小葱（葱白）shallot
蒜 garlic	小葱（葱末）chives
咖喱 curry	色拉油 salad oil
胡椒 pepper	香油 sesame oil
花椒 pepper corn/ Chinese prickly ash	大豆油 soy oil
	花生油 peanut oil
辣椒（大）chilly	橄榄油 olive oil
辣椒（小）pimiento	酱油 soy sauce
芝麻 sesame	醋 vinegar
面包渣 bread crumbs	料酒 Chinese yellow wine/ Shaoxing yellow wine
香菜 coriander/Chinese parsley	
淀粉 starch	黄酱 soy paste
嫩肉粉 tenderizer	甜面酱 sweet soy paste
蚝油 oyster sauce	鱼子酱 caviar
辣酱 chilly paste	鹅肝酱 goose liver paste
盐 salt	麻酱 sesame paste
糖 sugar	烤紫菜 baked nori
方糖 sugar cube	果酱 jam
冰糖 rock sugar/crystal sugar	黄油 butter
淀粉 starch	奶油 cream
	炼乳 condensed milk
	奶酪 cheese

蔬菜类 Veggies	
大白菜 Chinese leaves	豆角 bean
卷心菜 cabbage	土豆 potato
生菜 lettuce	山芋 yam
空心菜 water spinach	白薯 sweet potato
芥菜 gai choy	豌豆 pea
油菜 buk choy	茴香 fennel
菜心 choy sum	玉米 corn (cob)
泡菜 pickled veggie	藕 lotus root
茄子 eggplant/aubergine	苤蓝 swede/rutabaga
菜花 cauliflower	甜菜 beet
绿菜花 broccoli	胖白萝卜 parsnip
芥兰 Chinese broccoli	长白萝卜（大根）mooli/daikon
菠菜 spinach	樱桃萝卜 radish
芹菜 celery	胡萝卜 carrot
莴笋 lettuce leaves	水萝卜/心儿里美 turnip
芦笋 asparagus	竹笋 bamboo shoot
黄瓜 cucumber	木耳 black fungus
西葫芦 zucchini/courgette	银耳 white fungus
苦瓜 bitter cucumber	豆芽 bean sprout
节瓜/长冬瓜 squash	荸荠 water chestnut
丝瓜 towel cucumber	洋葱 onion
冬瓜 wax gourd	茶叶蛋/咸蛋 tea egg/salty egg
南瓜 pumpkin	松花蛋 (lime) preserved egg
番茄 tomato	蘑菇 mushroom
豆腐 tofu	球芽甘蓝 Brussels sprout
面筋 bean-curd dough	芸豆 kidney bean
朝鲜蓟 artichoke/globe artichoke	雪菜 pickle
甜椒 bell pepper/pepper	咸菜 brined vegetables

肉类 Meat	
鹌鹑 quail	鲫鱼 crucian carp
鸽子 pigeon	武昌鱼 blunt-snout bream
火鸡 turkey	胖头鱼 bighead
鸡 chicken	鲤鱼 carp
鸭 duck	草鱼 grass carp
鹅 goose	黄鱼 yellow croaker
肝 liver	鲍鱼 abalone
腿 leg	三文鱼 salmon
翅 wing	大马哈 dog salmon
爪 foot/claw	甲鱼 terrapin
猪肉 pork	鲶鱼 catfish
牛肉 beef	金枪 tuna
羊肉 mutton	泥鳅 loach
大排 stake	鲈鱼 bass
小排 rib	鳗 eel
里脊 fillet	比目鱼 flounder
百叶 stripe	鳎 sole
肚片 stomach	鲳 pomfret
腰花 kidney	鳕 cod
虾 shrimp	鲱 herring
对虾 prawn	河豚 globefish/balloon-fish
龙虾/小龙虾 lobster/crayfish	海参 sea cucumber
螃蟹 crab	蛤（蛏）clam
鱿鱼 squid	贝（青口）mussel
墨鱼 ink-fish	鱼翅 shark fin
章鱼 cuttlefish	海带 seaweed
桂鱼 Chinese perch	海蜇 jellyfish
黑鱼 snakehead	海胆 sea urchin

主食、小吃、甜品类 Dim Sum, Local Snacks & Desserts	
炒饭 fried rice	冰激凌 ice cream
面 noodle	奶昔 milk shake
春卷 spring roll	布丁 pudding
汤圆 glutinous rice ball	果冻 jelly
肠粉 vermicelli roll	饼干 biscuits
烧饼 pancake	曲奇饼 cookies
馒头 bun	巧克力 chocolate
油条 fried dough stick (ring/sheet)	酿皮 Shaanxi rice noodle
煎饼 fried waffle pancake	薯条 French fries
红豆 azuki	薯片 potato chips
粥羹 porridge/congee	腰果 cashew nut
汤汁 soup/juice	开心果 pistachio
饺子 dumpling	榛子 hazelnut
包子/烧卖 steamed dumpling	花生 peanut
馄饨 wonton	核桃 walnut
锅贴 fried dumpling	松子 pine nut
豆浆 soybean milk	栗子 chestnut
烤鸭 Peking roast duck	葵瓜子 sunflower seed
粽子 glutinous rice pyramid	南瓜子 pumpkin seed
绿豆 green mung bean	杏仁 almond
小米 millet	话梅 preserved prune
燕麦 oat	果脯 preserved fruit
糖葫芦 sugar-coated fruit crispy	鱼片/牛肉干/猪肉干 fish/beef/pork jerky
羊肉串 mutton kabab	方便面 instant noodle
肉夹馍/中式汉堡 Chinese hamburger	韩式泡菜 kimchi
掉渣饼 Chinese pizza	午餐肉/火腿三明治 luncheon meat/ham sandwich
寿司 sushi	

饮料、水果类 Beverage & Fruits	
红茶 black tea	啤酒 beer
绿茶 green tea	红酒 wine
乌龙茶 oolong tea	白酒 Chinese liquor
茉莉花茶 jasmine tea	香槟 champagne
菊花茶 chrysanthemum tea	酸奶 yoghurt
八宝茶 eight-flavor tea	可乐 cola
普洱茶 pu'er tea	雪碧 sprite
奶茶 milk tea	果汁 juice
香蕉 banana	百香果/西番莲 passion fruit
葡萄 grape	蔓越莓（橘）cranberry
柠檬 lemon	番石榴 guava
菠萝 pineapple	鳄梨/牛油果 avocado
西瓜 watermelon	山楂 hawthorn
苹果 apple	樱桃 cherry
哈密瓜 honey melon	桃子 peach
香瓜 melon	梨 pear
李子 plum	椰子 coconut
杏 apricot	草莓/蓝莓/黑莓 stawberry/blueberry/blackberry
青柠 lime	桑葚 mulberry
芒果 mango	猕猴桃 kiwi fruit
柚子 grapefruit	无花果 fig
榴莲 durian	山竹 mangosteen
荔枝/番荔枝 lychee/sugar apple	柿子 persimmon
木瓜 papaya	醋栗 gooseberry
橄榄 olive	枣 date
杨桃 starfruit	橘子 orange
枸杞 wolfberry	枇杷 loquat

Group Project

Please design a Chinese Dinner Tour Itineraries leaflet with your group members for the international tourists in Beijing. You need to prepare a 15-20 minutes' PPT presentation to display your findings, creations, imaginations and suggestions. The following procedure may be used as a reference.

Please discuss what kind of food may appeal to the international tourists, and fill in the recipe brainstorm worksheet below.

The following principles and suggestions may be helpful to your project work.

Group Size	Cold Dish	Main Dish	Side Dish	Staple food	Dissert	Beverage
Group Dinner For 9 – 16 people						
Party Dinner For 6 – 8 people						
Family Dinner For 3 – 5 people						
Couple's Dinner For 1 – 2 people						

Assignment 3 Role-play Tasks

Scenario 3 - A

Suppose you are guiding your tourists to take dinner at a restaurant specializing in Chinese local flavor. However they have big difficulty in reading the Chinese menu because all the dishes' names are written either in pinyin or in Chinese characters since the waiter/waitress has strong foreign/local accent. Please help them complete the ordering procedure by negotiating with the tourists. In your group there are one vegetarian, one with diabetes, and one allergic to alcohol. Please discuss with your group members and work out an economic Table D'hort menu fit for 10 tourists.

Your order should involve appetizers and cold dishes, main courses, staple food and desserts, beverages and drinks, and they should represent typical Chinese characteristics. Then please explain your order to your tourists especially on the ingredients and cooking skills.

The following Table D'hort menu may be used as a reference.

凉菜：四川泡菜，小葱拌豆腐，北京豆酱，大丰收

热菜：蚝油生菜，宫保鸡丁，黑椒牛柳，糖醋里脊，红烧狮子头，香菇油菜，西红柿炒鸡蛋

主菜：清蒸鲥鱼，北京烤鸭（选一）

汤：莲藕排骨汤

主食：金银馒头，炸酱面，扬州炒饭（选一）

甜品：马蹄绿豆沙，杏仁豆腐（选一）

酒水：矿泉水，菊花茶，山楂汁，果汁啤酒

Scenario 3 - B

Suppose you are guiding a group of student tourists to take some local snacks in the street. Please recommend some typical ones to them and explain the ingredients as well as how they are cooked. Then you go to visit a local family in Beijing. In the kitchen workshop, they are taught how to prepare and make the following dishes.

（1）Chinese dumplings

（2）Chinese hot-pot

Please role-play the workshop scenario with your group members. The following menu may be used as a reference.

小吃：小笼包，豆浆，小米粥，红豆粥，皮蛋瘦肉粥，煎饼，肉夹馍，褡裢火烧，馄饨，肠粉，汤圆，糖葫芦，羊肉串，炒粉，茶汤，鸡丝凉面，驴肉烧饼，年糕，粽子

厨艺工作室项目：白菜、韭菜、茴香馅饺子的制作

肥牛、羊肉火锅的制作

Scenario 3 - C

Laura is a thirteen year old girl who comes to Beijing with her school tour group. Today she and her school mates will visit a typical Beijing family living in a beautiful quadrangle courtyard. They will make and have dumpling lunch dinner in the host's home. As the tour guide, please teach them how to make dumplings and how to use chopsticks. In the evening they will go to Bian Yi Fang Restaurant to have the dinner of Peking Roast Duck, please teach them the proper table manners of eating Peking Roast Duck.

Unit 4

Scenario Warm-up 4 Shopping

Culture Interpretation 4 Souvenir

Assignment 4 Role-play Tasks

Scenario Warm-up 4 Shopping

Listening Extract 9

Listen to David selling in-flight duty-free to a passenger and answer the questions.

1. What size is the perfume bottle?
_____

2. How much is it in dollars?
_____

3. What types of cuddly toy are there?
_____

4. Which toy does the passenger buy?
_____

5. How much did the passenger spend in total?
_____

Listening Transcript for Extract 9

(Courtesy of Dubicka & O' Keeffe, English for International Tourism Pre-intermediate Students' Book, Unit 9, Exercise 12: 138–139)

David	Would you like any duty-free, madam?
Passenger A	Oh yes, I'd like to buy some perfume. Do you have any l'Eau d'Issey?
David	Yes, I think I do. I'll just get it for you. Here you are.
Passenger A	How much is it?
David	Let's see. It's the fifty milliliter bottle so that's twenty-nine pounds fifty, madam.
Passenger A	Can I pay in dollars?
David	Certainly, madam. But we only give change in pounds.
Passenger A	Oh, that's OK.
David	So that'll be forty-three dollars and thirty cents.
Passenger B	Shall we get something for Barbara's daughter?
Passenger A	That's a good idea. Do you have any soft toys?
David	Yes, there are two. I've got a leopard and a teddy bear — he's called Wilbur.
Passenger B	The Leopard looks cute.
Passenger A	It does, but I think I'll take the teddy bear.
David	So that's forty-three thirty for the perfume plus fourteen dollars sixty for the teddy. That makes fifty-seven ninety.
Passenger A	Here you are.
David	Thank you.

Listening Extract 10

Mr. and Mrs. O'Donnell talk to the receptionist at the Cape Grace Hotel.
Listen to their conversation and answer these questions.

1. What are Mr. and Mrs. O'Donnell going to do?
   _____

2. What does Beverley tell them not to take?
   _____

3. Where is Mr. O'Donnell going to leave his camera?
   _____

4. What advice does Beverley give them about their car?
   _____

5. Where does Beverley tell them not to go?
   _____

6. What does Mrs. O'Donnell want to visit?
   _____

Listening Transcript for Extract 10

(Courtesy of Dubicka & O'Keeffe, English for International Tourism Pre-intermediate Students' Book, Unit 7, Exercise 8: 136)

Robert	Hi, Bev, got my passport?
Beverley	Yes, Mr. O'Donnell. Here you are, sir.
Robert	We were thinking of going shopping in the city center for the afternoon. Is it safe?
Beverley	Yes, sir. You'll find that the center of Cape Town is no different from other major cities. You must take a few precautions, though. If you are going shopping, I recommend that you use traveler's check or credit cards. You shouldn't take large amount of cash. The markets are very crowded and lively but beware of pickpockets.
Robert	Is that so? What about the camera?
Beverley	You should try not to attract attention to yourself by carrying cameras and wearing expensive jewellery.
Leeta	Sounds like we'd better leave our things in the safe deposit box in our room, honey.
Robert	You're right, Leeta. We'll do that. Hey, now where did I put those car keys?
Beverley	If you are driving, sir, you must keep your car doors locked at all times.
Robert	This is like being back home in Chicago!
Beverley	One last thing, avoid walking around the poorer areas of the city.
Leeta	How about going to see Robben Island?
Beverley	There are several ferries but it's best to book with an organized tour of the island. I can reserve you places for you here at the hotel. Oh, and another thing, it's a good idea to take a pill if you get seasick easily.
Robert	Thanks Bev, you've been very helpful.

Culture Interpretation 4 Souvenir

Vocabulary Workshop

What kind of typical souvenirs could you think of? Then please translate the following words into English.

1. 珐琅	2. 景泰蓝	3. 水晶	4. 玉石	5. 玛瑙
6. 琥珀	7. 象牙	8. 珍珠	9. 钻石	10. 珊瑚
11. 耳钉/耳环	12. 手镯	13. 胸针/胸花	14. 吊坠/项链	15. 发夹/发卡
16. 领带夹	17. 袖扣	18. 首饰盒	19. 铜	20. 青铜/黄铜
21. 铂金	22. 银	23. 黄金	24. 毛笔	25. 墨
26. 宣纸	27. 砚台	28. 文房四宝	29. 书法	30. 国画
31. 印章	32. 笔筒	33. 镇纸	34. 笔架	35. 内画壶
36. 陶	37. 瓷	38. 紫砂	39. 陶艺	40. 根雕
41. 盆景	42. 泥人	43. 面塑	44. 绢人	45. 双面绣
46. 汉字	47. 漆雕	48. 年画	49. 蜡染	50. 剪纸
51. 风车	52. 拨浪鼓	53. 不倒翁	54. 中国结	55. 麻将
56. 风筝	57. 毽子	58. 空竹	59. 鲁班锁	60. 九连环

Group Project

Please design a ***Souvenir Pack*** with your group members for the international tourists. You need to prepare a 20-30 minutes' PPT presentation to display your findings, creations, imaginations and suggestions. The following procedure may be used as a reference.

1. Please discuss what kinds of souvenirs may appeal to the international tourists, and fill in the needs analysis worksheet below. For each grid, please think of at least three items.

Needs Analysis Worksheet

Age	For Male	For Female
3 – 6		
7 – 11		
12 – 17		
18 – 25		
26 – 35		
36 – 49		
50 – 69		
70 – 100		

2. Please think about why these items may be attractive to the tourists and if there are appropriate souvenir products in the market. Try to find some pictures from the Internet and write brief introductions about your findings.

3. Please discuss with your group members about in what aspects our domestic souvenir design could be improved compared with the international mature designs and why.

4. Please discuss what kind of criteria should be observed in the design work and try to put forward some specific suggestions about the souvenir product design for our domestic producers, your imagination and creation are extremely encouraged.

5. Prepare your PPT file together and share the presentation task.

Assignment 4 Role-play Tasks

Scenario 4 - A

Wu Min (the local guide), Zhang Yong (the national guide) and Julia Wong (the escort) are waiting for the tourists at the souvenir shop. Three tourists turn to them for help because the shop assistants can't communicate with them effectively. Then they have to translate for them.

Scenario 4 - A - 1

Ms. Greenwood enjoys Chinese new year paintings very much. Shop assistant A recommends four paintings to her and tells them the symbolic meanings, the background stories of each one (五子登科、和合二仙、刘海戏金蟾、年年有余), but the shop assistant's English is too hard to understand that Ms. Greenwood can't make a decision. Then the local guide comes to translate for her and she is able to make the final decision.

Hints & Clues

五子登科	和合二仙	刘海戏金蟾	年年有余
Five Promising Boys	Immortals of Harmony & Union	Game between Liuhai and Froggy Bank	Affluent New Year

Scenario 4 - A - 2

Mr. Sealer wants to buy some Chinese toys for his three grandchildren who are interested in math, arts and sports respectively. Shop assistant B recommends the following six toys for him (九连环、鲁班锁、空竹、毽子、风筝、中国结) but can't explain to him effectively about how to play the toys. At that time his national guide comes to help him and Mr. Sealer feels quite satisfied with some of the toys and purchases three different pieces for all his three grandchildren respectively.

Hints & Clues

九连环	鲁班锁	空竹	毽子	风筝	中国结
Chinese Rings	Luban Smart Lock	Chinese yo-yo	Chinese Shuttlecock	Kite	Chinese Knot

Scenario 4 - A - 3

Miss. Whitman plans to send a wedding gift for her cousin and she is quite interested in the Chinese paper-cut since her cousin is a stage designer. The shop assistant C recommends four pieces to her (福、龙凤呈祥、鸳鸯戏水、年年有余) but she can't understand the Chinese introduction remarks. The escort (a Chinese American) sees the situation and goes to help her.

Hints & Clues

福	龙凤呈祥	鸳鸯戏水	年年有余
Blessing	Harmonious Union of Dragon & Phoenix	Mandarin Ducks' Marriage	Affluent New Year

Please prepare three dialogues based on the foregoing scenarios and then role-play them in front of your classmates.

New Year's Paintings

Unit 4

Chinese Toys & Handicraft

Chinese Paper-cuts

Scenario 4 - B

Mr. Hutchinson is a retired shop manager from the States. He comes to China for the first time. He plans to buy some souvenirs for his wife, his daughter, his daughter-in-law and his grandson. Discuss with your group members about what will happen in the real-life situations and what suggestions you could provide him as a tour guide. Then role-play the solutions you have made up in terms of your discussion. In this short play, 3 roles will be involved, namely the Chinese salesperson, Mr. Hutchinson, as well as the tour guide as the translator.

Scenario 4 - C

Miss Campton is a landlady who owns many properties for let to the oversea students in U.K. Currently she is taking her holiday in China and this is also her first time to Beijing. She plans to take some gifts back to some old neighbors, some friends working at church, and her relatives. Of course these might not be expensive but should be something typical Chinese. In addition, she also needs to buy something for herself as a valuable souvenir. As a guide, please recommend something to her, and role-play the situation with your group members. In this task, 3 roles are required: the Chinese sales person, the guide and Miss Campton.

Scenario 4 - D

Ms. Hellene found some defect in her new-bought toy panda yesterday at the souvenir shop and would like to change a new one today. Since she can't speak Chinese, she asks Miss Wang (the guide) to be her translator. However, when they go there, the sales person tells her it is the last panda in the shop and there is no more available. After negotiation, Ms. Hellene gets her refund. To console her dissatisfaction, Miss Wang suggests her buying a set of Olympic Mascots. Ms. Hellene accepts the advice finally.

Unit 5

Scenario Warm-up 5 Travel Inquiry & Booking

Culture Interpretation 5 Auspicious Fauna and Flora

Assignment 5 Role-play Tasks

Scenario Warm-up 5 Travel Inquiry & Booking

Listening Extract 11

Listen to the telephone conversation between Mr. Gould and a travel agent and make necessary changes to the booking form below.

	PTC0189-02
	Pacific Travel Company
Name	Mr. Stuart Gould
Tour title	2-day Mount Cook National Park Tour
Number of passengers	14
Accommodation	Mount Cook Motel
	7 double rooms
Departure date	23 March, 8:20 a.m.
Departure point	Newmans Terminal, Christchurch

Listening Transcript for Extract 11

(Courtesy of Dubicka & O'Keeffe, English for International Tourism Pre-intermediate Students' Book, Unit 11, Exercise 5: 139–140)

Nathalie	Pacific Travel Company, Nathalie speaking. How can I help you?
Stuart	Hello, it's Stuart Gould here. I've booked a two-day group tour with your company and I need to make some changes to the original booking.
Nathalie	Certainly, Mr. Gould. Do you have your confirmation form with you?
Stuart	Yes, it's PTC... PTC0189 dash 02.
Nathalie	PTC0189 dash 02. That's a two day Mount Cook National Park Tour for a party of fourteen, departing on 23rd March. What changes would you like to make?
Stuart	We'd prefer to go a day later, on 24th March. Is that possible? We're staying an extra day in Queenstown on the 23rd.
Nathalie	Just let me check, Mr. Gould. Yes, that's now confirmed. The coach leaves at 8:20 a.m. from Newmans Terminal in Christchurch.
Stuart	I'm sorry, could you repeat that, please?
Nathalie	Certainly, the coach leaves at 8:20 a.m. from Newmans Terminal.
Stuart	Thanks. And another thing, there are now only thirteen of us, so we'll need five double rooms and one triple room.
Nathalie	OK, Mr. Gould, I'll make that change for you.
Stuart	Also, can you tell me what time the bus returns to Christchurch?
Nathalie	The coach arrives back in Christchurch at approximately 6:15 p.m.
Stuart	Ah, you see we're flying to Auckland the following day to catch a connecting flight home to Scotland, so we're hoping to get a good night's sleep.
Nathalie	The coach service is generally very punctual, Mr. Gould. I'm sure there'll be no problem.
Stuart	Oh, good.
Nathalie	Now I'll just confirm those changes. That's a group of thirteen,

for the two-day Mount Cook National Park Tour, departing from Newmans Terminal at 8:20 a.m. on Tuesday 24th March. The motel accommodation at Mount Cook is five double rooms and one triple room.

Stuart   Yes, that's right.
Nathalie   I'll send you a fax today to confirm those changes, Mr. Gould.
Stuart   Goodbye and thank you very much for your help, Nathalie.
Nathalie   You're welcome. Goodbye Mr. Gould.

Listening Extract 12

Listen to someone making a holiday booking over the telephone. Note the details of the travelers, their trip and payments. After you have listened, work out the sum of the money the caller will write on the check.

Intourist

PLEASE USE BLOCK CAPITALS
BOOKING REFERENCE   UKR352. JP
TOUR NUMBER   _____
DEPARTURE DATE   _____
DEPARTURE AIRPORT   _____
TOTAL HOLIDAY PRICE _____

Mr./Mrs. Ms./Miss	First Name	Surname	Address	Tel. No.	Nationality

INSURANCE	PAYMENT
Insurance is compulsory on an Intourist Travel Limited holiday. We assume you require our Insurance UNLESS you have made alternative arrangements for greater or comparable cover.	Deposit of £100 per fare-paying passenger or full payment when travel is within 8 weeks. Insurance premium per person £ _____ Visa per person £ _____ Deposit per person £ _____ If payment is made by credit card, the credit card charge form must be completed.
VISA SERVICE	**TOTAL**
A visa is compulsory. The visa charge will automatically be added to the invoice. Please fill in the standard application form.	I warrant that I am authorized to make this booking. I have read and agree to abide by the booking conditions and other information set out in the brochure relevant to my holiday. Signature:

Listening Transcript for Extract 12

(Courtesy of Jacob & Strutt, English for International Tourism Post-Intermediate Students' Book, Unit 5 Listening 2: 118)

Travel Agent	Good morning, Intourist, can I help you?
Maughan	Hello, er yes, can I speak to Natasha, please?
Travel Agent	Er, yes, who's calling?
Maughan	I spoke to her last week about a holiday in the Ukraine and I'd like to make a booking.
Travel Agent	OK, could you hold on please? I'll put you through to her desk.
Maughan	Thank you...
Natasha	Hello.
Maughan	Is that Natasha?
Natasha	Speaking.
Maughan	Um, I visited your agency last week and we talked about the tours you organize in Ukraine. You said I should get in touch with you if I'd made up my mind.
Natasha	Oh yes, I remember. Have you decided where you'd like to go?
Maughan	Yes, I'd like to make a booking if that's OK.
Natasha	Fine. I'll just get a booking form. Hold the line... Right. Could you tell me which tour you've decided on?
Maughan	The one — sorry, I haven't got the reference with me — the ten-day one to Moscow via Odessa. We fly from Gatwick.
Natasha	OK, I'll look up the reference number later. Can you tell me what date you want to leave on?
Maughan	The thirteenth of July.
Natasha	Fine. So would you mind giving me your name, please?
Maughan	It's for me and my wife — Mr. and Mrs. Maughan.
Natasha	How is that spelt?
Maughan	M-A-U-G-H-A-N.

Natasha	And please could I have your first names?
Maughan	Linda and Kevin.
Natasha	Is that Linda with an "i" or "ay"?
Maughan	An "I". It's L-I-N-D-A.
Natasha	Thank you, and I'll need your home address.
Maughan	Certainly. That's 41, Swynford Hill, Temple Fortune, London, NW11 7PN.
Natasha	41, I'm sorry, could you please spell Swynford for me?
Maughan	Of course, S-W-Y-N-F-O-R-D. Then Hill, Temple Fortune, London, NW11 7PN.
Natasha	And the telephone number?
Maughan	0181 392 4535.
Natasha	And do you have a number at work?
Maughan	Yes, 0171 274 0083, extension 32.
Natasha	Thanks. And are you both British?
Maughan	I am, my wife has an Irish passport.
Natasha	Right, now do you mind if I just check the details? It's Mr. Kevin Maughan spelt M-A-U-G-H-A-N and Mrs. Linda Maughan of 41, Swynford Hill, Temple Fortune, London, NW11 7BN.
Maughan	Sorry, could you repeat that?
Natasha	Mr. Kevin M...
Maughan	No, the last bit of the postcode. Did you say P or B?
Natasha	B. B for Bravo.
Maughan	No, it's P for... for er... Peter.
Natasha	Sorry, thanks. So it's London, NW11 7PN. Telephone number 0181 392 4535 and at work 0171 274 0083, extension 32. Departure date 13th July. Now, there's the insurance which is... er... is compulsory on this kind of tour. Would you like to make your own arrangements or would you rather take out the standard insurance policy?
Maughan	Oh... I guess the standard one. It saves a lot of trouble.

Natasha	Yes. OK. Well, the insurance premium is... wait a minute, I'll look in the brochure... um (reads to herself). It's for ten days, isn't it? "Up to eight days, £19. Nine to twelve days £22 per person". Right, so that's £22 per person. And... um... you'll need a visa as well.
Maughan	OK, um... do you know how much that costs?
Natasha	Yes, that will be an additional £17 per person. Shall I look after that or would you prefer to get it yourself?
Maughan	No, no, you do it! I haven't got time!
Natasha	Right, so I'll need you to fill in an application form and I'll also need three passport size photos and a copy of the inside cover of your passport, so if you bring those in the next time you drop in I'll send everything off with the confirmation.
Maughan	OK.
Natasha	And I'll also need your deposit which is £100 a head.
Maughan	Right, well I'll drop by at the beginning of next week and make you out a check then.
Natasha	Good, thank you for calling. Goodbye.

Listening Extract 13

A travel agent deals with a telephone enquiry about Florida. Listen and complete the reservation form below.

Special Offers

US fly-drive holidays

Florida 7 nts and 14 nts

from £399

Tel. World Breaks

0207946004

World Breaks

Reservations

Type of holiday:	US fly-drive
Resort name:	Orlando
Type of accommodation:	(1)
Number of nights:	(2)
Out date:	(3)
Departure airport:	LHR
Return date:	(4)
Departure airport:	ORL
Number of adults:	(5)
Names:	(6)
Number of children:	(7)
Name(s):	(8)

Listening Transcript for Extract 13

(Courtesy of Dubicka & O'Keeffe, English for International Tourism Pre-intermediate Students' Book, Unit 2, Exercise 2: 132)

Travel Agent   Good afternoon, World Breaks, Janet Cookson speaking. How can I help you?

Caller   Hello, I saw your advert in the newspaper for fly-drive holidays in Florida. Does that mean you get flights, accommodation and car hire all included in the price?

Travel Agent   That's right, madam.

Caller   And what kind of accommodation is it?

Travel Agent   Well, there are two options. You can have a self-catering apartment or stay in a hotel.

Caller   We'd prefer an apartment, I think. How much will it cost for two weeks?

Travel Agent   That all depends on when you travel. When are you thinking of going, madam?

Caller   Well, some time when it's quieter, the second half of May. Is it off-season then?

Travel Agent   Yes, it is. That's a very good time to go. We have a great offer at the moment: fourteen nights' fly-drive with self-catering apartments for £543 per person.

Caller   That sounds good. Could I book it now?

Travel Agent   Certainly. Let me see, the flights are from London Heathrow on Thursdays, so that's Thursday 17th May, returning from Orlando, Florida on the morning of Thursday 31st May. How does that sound?

Caller   That's fine.

Travel Agent   Could I have the names of the people travelling, please?

Caller   There's me, Janet Wright, my husband Simon and our son Andrew.

Travel Agent   Could you spell your surname for me, Mrs. Wright?

Caller   Yes, that's W-R-I-G-H-T.

Travel Agent	Ok, thank you. Just let me confirm the details. That's three people, two adults and one child, leaving London Heathrow on Thursday 17th May, returning on Thursday 31st May.
Caller	Yes, that's right.
Travel Agent	Thank you, Mrs. Wright. Now how do you wish to pay for your holiday? By credit card?

Listening Extract 14

Listen to four enquires at the Dublin TIC. Which of the following places are recommended? What kind of sights are they?

Newgrange, Dublinia, Museum of Modern Art, Dublin Civic Museum, St. Stephen's Green, Parnell Square, O'Donoghue's

Tourist Attraction	What's it special for?
1	
2	
3	
4	

Listening Transcript for Extract 14

(Courtesy of Strutt, English for International Tourism Intermediate Students' Book, Unit 8, Exercise 10: 137)

Part One

Visitor Hello, we've got two small children and they're getting a bit fed up with historic monuments and museums. Is there anything that might be suitable for them?

Receptionist How old are they?

Visitor Ten and twelve.

Receptionist Well, why don't you take them to the zoo?

Visitor Where is it?

Receptionist It's only about three kilometers from the city center in the grounds of Phoenix Park. I'll give you a map if you like. Alternatively, you might like to think about going to Dublinia.

Visitor Oh yes, what's that?

Receptionist It's a multimedia exhibition of medieval Dublin. It's great. The kids can dress up in costumes and it has all the sounds and smells of the time. It's open daily from ten till five.

Receptionist Sounds kind of fun. How do we get there?

Receptionist You walk along Dame Street and it's just behind the Cathedral.

Visitor OK, thank you very much.

Part Two

Visitor Hello. I've seen pretty much everything there is to see in Dublin itself and I was wondering what there is to do further afield.

Receptionist Do you have a car?

Visitor Yes.

Receptionist Well how about going to Newgrange?

Visitor What is Newgrange?

Receptionist It's a prehistoric site which is about 5,000 years old. It's a burial chamber and the oldest solar observatory in the world. It's very impressive.
Visitor Have you got a leaflet?
Receptionist Sure.
Visitor How far away is it?
Receptionist It's about fifty or sixty kilometers.
Visitor How do I get there?
Receptionist Basically, you take the N2 road heading north out of the city towards a town called Slane in County Meath. Then you turn right about two miles south of Slane and Newgrange Visitors' Centre is sign-posted. But if I were you, I'd get there early because it gets very crowded in summer and there can be long queues. Your best bet is to get there at about ten o'clock in the morning.
Visitor OK, thanks, I'll give it a try.

Part Three

Visitor Good morning, I'm staying here a few days and I'm interested in Irish literature. Can you tell me the best places to go?
Receptionist Is this your first visit?
Visitor Yes.
Receptionist OK, well I suggest starting off with the Dublin Writers Museum — here's a brochure. You can see manuscripts and letters and rare editions of people like Jonathan Swift or Oscar Wilde. And then if you like James Joyce, there's the James Joyce Cultural Center.
Visitor Where is the Writer's Museum?
Receptionist It's at number 18 Parnell Square in the north of the city. Have you got a car?
Visitor Yes.
Receptionist Well, here, I'll give you a map. If you see here, you cross the river, the

	best thing is to go over Grattan Bridge at the end of Parliament Street, that's here. Go up Capel Street to the end and fork right into Bolton Street. Then it's the third on the right into Granby Row and it's on the left just here. It's opposite the Museum of Modern Art. You can't miss it.
Visitor	OK. Thank you very much. You've been very helpful.

Part Four

Receptionist	Hello. Can you tell me where the best sort of traditional Irish pub is around here, you know with traditional music and that kind of stuff?
Visitor	If you're into Irish folk music then O'Donoghue's is probably the best. That's where the Dubliner's group started up.
Receptionist	Oh right, great. Can you tell us where it is?
Visitor	It's in Merrion Row, just off St Stephen's Green.
Receptionist	St. Stephen's Green? Where is that?
Visitor	I'll show you on the map. It's here, in this square E5, just between St Stephen's Green and Baggott Street.
Receptionist	Right thanks. I'll go there this evening.

Listening Extract 15

Listen to a hotel receptionist recommending places to visit in Cracow and answer the questions.

1. Why hasn't Laura got much time for sightseeing?
   _____

2. How long will it take to see the sights at the Wawel Castle?
   _____

3. Why does the receptionist recommend going early to the castle?
   _____

4. What type of places is Pod Baranami?
   _____

5. Why doesn't Laura want to go there?
   _____

6. What does Laura decide to do in the evening?
   _____

Listening Transcript for Extract 15

(Courtesy of Dubicka & O'Keeffe, English for International Tourism Pre-intermediate Students' Book, Unit 10, Exercise 8–9: 139)

Laura	Excuse me, I've been attending the conference here and tomorrow. I've got a free day to do some sightseeing. Do you have any information about the city?
Receptionist	Yes, of course. What kind of information do you need exactly?
Laura	You know, places to visit, but I haven't got much time because I'm flying back to the UK on Sunday night.
Receptionist	Let me see. How about visiting the Wawel Castle?
Laura	Oh yes, my colleague said it's worth a visit.
Receptionist	That's right. There's the castle, the cathedral and a cave. You must see the Dragon's Cave.
Laura	And how long do you think it'll take to see everything?
Receptionist	You'll probably need about three hours to see it all. Walking around the gardens takes some time.
Laura	OK, that's a whole morning then.
Receptionist	But, you should get there early because there are always very long queues.
Laura	Oh, right. Oh, and one more thing. Are there any nice cafés or bars nearby?
Receptionist	Well, the market square has lots of cafés and cellar bars. You know, bars underground.
Laura	Really? Can you recommend one?
Receptionist	Why don't you go to Pod Baranami?
Laura	What's it like?
Receptionist	It's famous for its cabarets, they also have a disco in the evenings.
Laura	What time does the disco start?
Receptionist	About 8:00 p.m..

Laura	I don't know, I don't really want to go dancing this evening.
Receptionist	What about jazz? Do you like jazz?
Laura	Oh, I love jazz.
Receptionist	You could go to the pub, U Louisa. There's live jazz or blues music on Wednesdays.
Laura	Sounds great. I think I'll go there in the evening. Thanks.

Tour Booking Procedure

1. Ask the client to sign the booking form.
2. Collect deposit payment.

2a. If the client pays in cash or by cheque, issue the receipt and forward the payment to the tour operator concerned.

2b. If the client pays by credit card, make sure the credit card section on the booking form is completed and signed.

3. Deal with insurance.

3a. If the TOs' insurance is chosen, add the premium to the deposit.

3b. If the client takes out his/her own insurance, noting this on the booking form.

4. Send off booking form to TO for confirmation.

4a. If the expiry date is imminent, then telephone and make arrangement to extend the option.

4b. Make a note of the date when receiving the confirmation or the invoice.

5. Make a note of when the client should make a full payment.
6. When confirmation is received, there are two things you can do.

6a. Check all important details.

6b. Highlight the latest date for payment and send it to the client.

Culture Interpretation 5 Auspicious Fauna and Flora

Vocabulary Workshop

Please translate the following auspicious animals and plants into English.

1. 松树	2. 竹	3. 梅花	4. 兰花	5. 柳树
6. 杨树	7. 侧柏	8. 龙柏	9. 槐树	10. 国槐/龙爪槐
11. 樟木	12. 檀香木	13. 紫檀/花梨	14. 红木	15. 楠木
16. 桃花	17. 合欢	18. 荷花/芙蓉	19. 睡莲	20. 菊花
21. 桂花	22. 美人蕉	23. 石榴	24. 寿桃	25. 蟠桃
26. 牡丹	27. 枣	28. 栗子	29. 花生	30. 核桃
31. 珙桐	32. 人参	33. 灵芝	34. 油菜花	35. 金丝猴
36. 小熊猫	37. 娃娃鱼	38. 海龟	39. 玳瑁	40. 大熊猫
41. 麒麟	42. 虎	43. 豹	44. 象	45. 獬豸
46. 龙	47. 狮子	48. 水牛	49. 黄牛	50. 梅花鹿
51. 蟾蜍	52. 八哥	53. 鹦鹉	54. 黄鹂	55. 鸳鸯
56. 孔雀	57. 鸿雁	58. 仙鹤	59. 燕子	60. 飞燕/百灵
61. 凤凰	62. 喜鹊	63. 蝙蝠	64. 金鱼	65. 鲤鱼

1 Chinese & Western Zodiac

What does the Chinese zodiac refer to? Could you please explain why they appear in such order? Which sign of the zodiac were you born under? How long does a cycle of the Chinese zodiac occur in?

1	2	3	4	5	6
7	8	9	10	11	12

鼠 **Year of the Mouse** 1972, 1984, 1996, 2008 Mouse people are very popular. They like to invent things and are good artists.	牛 **Year of the Ox** 1973, 1985, 1997, 2009 People born in this year are dependable and calm. They are good listeners and have very strong ideas.	虎 **Year of the Tiger** 1974, 1986, 1998, 2010 Tiger people are brave. Other people respect tiger people for their deep thoughts and courageous actions.	兔 **Year of the Rabbit** 1975, 1987, 1999, 2011 People born in this year are nice to be around. They like to talk, and many people trust them.
龙 **Year of the Dragon** 1976, 1988, 2000, 2012 Dragon people have good health and lots of energy. They are good friends because they listen carefully to others.	蛇 **Year of the Snake** 1977, 1989, 2001, 2013 People born in this year love good books, food, music, and plays. They will have good luck with money.	马 **Year of the Horse** 1978, 1990, 2002, 2014 People born in this year are popular, cheerful, and are quick to compliment others. Horse people can work very hard.	羊 **Year of the Goat** 1979, 1991, 2003, 2015 People born in this year are very good artists. They ask many questions, like nice things, and are very wise.
猴 **Year of the Monkey** 1980, 1992, 2004, 2016 Monkey people are very funny. They can always make people laugh. They are also very good problem solvers.	鸡 **Year of the Rooster** 1981, 1993, 2005, 2017 People born in this year are hard wokers. They have many talents and think deep thoughts.	狗 **Year of the Dog** 1982, 1994, 2006, 2018 Dog people are loyal and can always keep a secret. Sometimes dog people worry too much.	猪 **Year of the Pig** 1983, 1995, 2007, 2019 People born in this year are very good students. They are honest and brave. They always finish a project or assignment.

Can you identify the following western zodiac signs? Please match the Greek terms with correct signs and English words from the random-arranged choices below.

1 Aries	2 Taurus	3 Gemini	4 Cancer	5 Leo	6 Virgo
7 Libra	8 Scorpio	9 Sagittarius	10 Capricorn	11 Aquarius	12 Pisces

Signs

♍ ♑ ♏ ♒

♉ ♋ ♌ ♎

♈ ♓ ♊ ♐

Zodiac

Horned goat

Twins

Crab

Ram

Fish

Lion

Virgin

Scales

Water Bearer

Archer

Bull

Scorpion

Western Zodiac

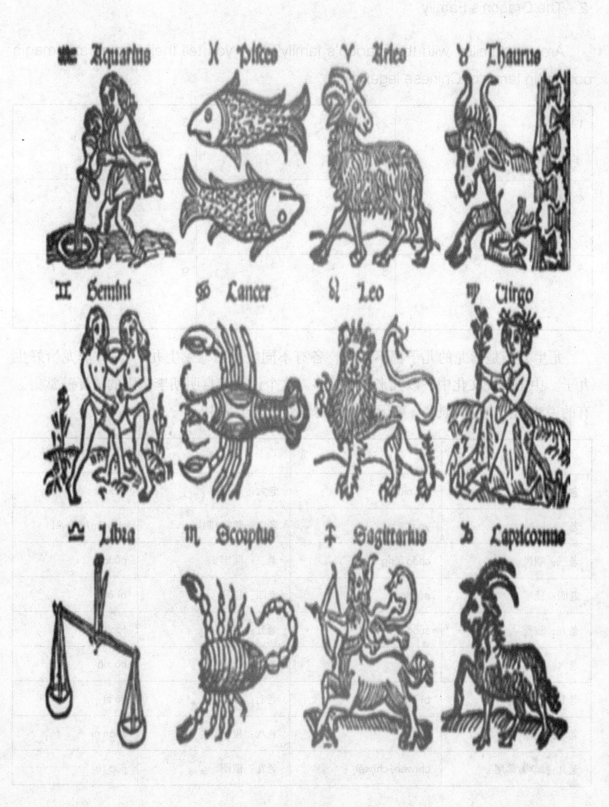

2 The Dragon's Family

Are you familiar with the dragon's family? Can you tell their names and magic powers in terms of Chinese legend?

1	2	3
4	5	6
7	8	9

龙生九子是指龙的儿子都不是龙，各有不同。所谓"龙生九子"，并非龙恰好生九子。中国传统文化中，以九来表示极多。这个说法来自明朝李东阳的《怀麓堂集》。有的说法还把螭首、麒麟、朝天犼、貔貅也列入龙子之中。

李东阳版本	读音	民间版本	读音
老大：囚牛	qiú niú	老大：赑屃	bì xì
老二：睚眦	yá zì	老二：鸱吻/鸱尾	chīwěn/chīwěi
老三：嘲风	cháo fēng	老三：蒲牢	pú láo
老四：蒲牢	pú láo	老四：狴犴	bì àn
老五：狻猊	suān ní	老五：饕餮	tāo tiè
老六：赑屃	bì xì	老六：蚣蝮	bà xià
老七：狴犴	bì àn	老七：睚眦	yá zì
老八：负屃	fù xì	老八：狻猊	suān ní
老九：螭吻/鸱尾	chīwěn/chīwěi	老九：椒图	jiāo tú

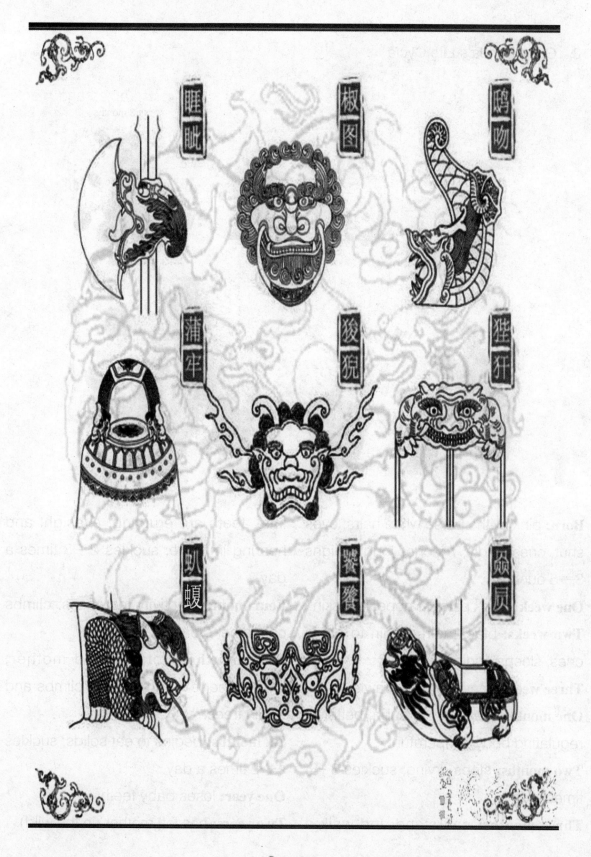

3 Giant Panda's Life Cycle

Born: pink, with sparse white hairs; eyes shut, cries loudly; 7 inches long; weighs 3—5 ounces.

One week: black patches appear on skin.

Two weeks: black hairs begin to grow; cries, sleeps and suckles.

Three weeks: may begin to crawl.

One month: eyes start to open; better at regulating body temperature.

Two months: stops crying; suckles 3—4 times a day.

Three months: can stand and walk a little; teeth are erupting; eyesight and hearing improve; suckles 2—3 times a day.

Four months: activity increases; climbs on mother's back to play.

Five months: trots behind mother; imitates her eating bamboo; climbs and sits in trees.

Six months: begins to eat solids; suckles 1—2 times a day.

One year: loses baby teeth.

Two years: has left mother (in the wild).

Group Project

1. Suppose you are going to nominate a mascot for an International Tour Culture Festival.

2. You are asked to nominate 10 candidates (5 animals and 5 plants) with auspicious symbolic meanings in the Chinese culture and give your reasons.

3. Then please find at least 5 animals which are popular with westerners but not accepted in the traditional Chinese culture and give your reasons.

4. Please prepare your project in the following procedure.

5. Discuss what five aspects of the Chinese culture you are going to display to the international tourists.

6. Decide what animals and plants will be the top-ten candidates in your presentation.

7. Find 3 reasons for each candidate.

8. Decide what animals are not appropriate to be the candidates but could be widely accepted by westerners.

9. Find 3 reasons for each animal.

10. Share your preparation work among your group members.

11. Produce your PPT slides individually.

12. Put your slides together and arrange them in good order.

13. Print out your PPT slides in the handout format (every 6 slides in one page) and hand it in on the day of presentation.

Please refer to the following worksheet to initiate your project work discussion.

Cultural Symbol	Candidates	Reasons
1	1	1
		2
		3
Cultural Symbol	Inappropriate Animals	Reasons
1	.	1
		2
		3

Assignment 5 Role-play Tasks

Scenario 5 - A

Suppose you work in the Tourist Information Center at Jade Palace Hotel in Beijing. One day some tourists come to enquire about their self-access city tours. Please make some recommendations to them.

Scenario 5 - A - 1 A couple with their two young daughters participate in a package tour in Beijing. However they don't like Peking Opera performance and Tea House Dinner arranged tomorrow, so they come to enquiry about some information on local snacks. Please recommend some restaurants with local flavors to them and show them how to go there.	**Scenario 5 - A - 2** Two oversea students of Chinese Martial Arts at CUPES (Capital University of Physical Education and Sports) come to enquire some shopping information because they want to buy some gifts for their families. Please recommend some shopping malls, streets, supermarkets to them and show them how to go there.
Scenario 5 - A - 3 An old British couple working at Renmin University come to ask some information of the city attractions. Since they have already visited the popular ones like the Forbidden City, the Summer Palace and the Temple of Heaven, please recommend some other places worthy of seeing that they have never been to. Finally, please tell them how to go there.	**Scenario 5 - A - 4** Three amateur photographers come to enquire about the places where the local people's happy life can be fully reflected. The aspects they are interested in are the schools, the neighborhood's activities, the shopping people, as well as the people at the entertainment or catering sites. Please recommend some places to them and tell them how to go there.

Scenario 5 - B

Scenario 5 - B - 1

Mrs. Susan Fishman adopted her Chinese daughter — Nancy 10 years ago. This autumn she plans to take Nancy to China with her husband for 2 weeks, so she come to your company to make some inquiries about her trip. Please provide some advices for her.

Cue card

For Susan	For Consultant A
1. Where to go?	
2. What route?	
3. What to see?	
4. Why attractive?	
5. More details about Beijing.	

Scenario 5 - B - 2

After negotiating with her family, Susan telephones your company to book her trip to China. Please help her to fill in the booking form and check her personal information. You may refer to the format of booking form in the previous handouts.

Cue Card

For Susan	For Consultant A
1. How much?	1. How long?
2. How and when to confirm?	2. Number of pax? (name, gender, age, relations)
	3. When?
	4. Want insurance?

Scenario 5 - B - 3

Susan telephones your company again to change her booking last month for some private reasons. Her former consultant is on business leave and another colleague takes over the recording job.

Cue Card

For Susan	For Consultant B
1. She has to delay the trip for one week because Mr. Dick Fishman has to attend a company conference. 2. Her mother Linda Hopkin (70 years old) will join them and stay with Nancy. 3. Nancy wants to see pandas in Beijing.	

Unit 6

Scenario Warm-up 6 Itinerary Negotiation

Culture Interpretation 6 Folklores and Lengendary Figures

Assignment 6 Role-play Tasks

Scenario Warm-up 6 Itinerary Negotiation

Please read the following two itineraries and translate them into Chinese.

Supplementary Reading Extract 2

<u>Cuba Tour</u>

Day 1

Depart London mid-morning Tuesday on VIASA via Caracas. Arrival late evening in Havana. Direct to the Hotel Plaza, opposite Central Park in old Havana, the area famed for its old Spanish Days.

Days 2 - 3

Explore Havana. Visit to a handicraft centre and the Guanabacoa museum on the outskirts of Havana, which has rooms dedicated to the influence of African cultures on Cuba. Free time to wander the streets of old Havana and appreciate the city's fine architecture. Visit to the Museum of the Revolution, the old fort and the Cathedral.

Day 4

Visit to a cigar factory. Transfer to the airport for flight to Santiago de Cuba in the east of the island, famed for its buildings and beautiful settings. Overnight staying in Las Americas hotel.

Day 5

City tour, including the Moncada barracks which Fidel Castro and a group of followers failed to storm in 1953 in an early abortive attempt to seize power. Good museums in Santiago include the Casa Velazquez dating back to the 16th century and the Museo Bacardi (Optional).

Day 6

Excursion to the Basilica in El Cobre, a village 18 miles northern of Santiago.

Transfer to airport and return to Havana. Accommodation in the Plaza Hotel.

Day 7

Return home.

Supplementary Reading Extract 3

ICELAND Outline Itinerary

Thursday: Evening flight from London Heathrow to Keflavik. Transfer on arrival to Hotel Island in Reykjavik.

Friday: Morning city Sight-seeing Tour and afternoon to explore or shop at leisure.

Saturday: (New Year's Eve): Late morning excursion to the Blue Lagoon to bathe in its milky blue waters. Evening Viking-style banquet. Just before midnight firework display. See the New Year in with a celebratory glass of Brennivin (Icelandic Schnapps).

Sunday: (New Year's Day): The Golden Circle — a full day tour. Leaving Reykjavik we travel over Hellisheidi Pass to Hveragerdi, the "greenhouse village" where fruit, vegetables and flowers are grown in green houses heated by geothermal water. Visit to the Great Geysir, after which all others are named. Drive to Gullfoss, considered by many to be Iceland's most beautiful waterfall. Cascading in two stages into a spectacular 15 km gorge, the falls are often partly frozen at this time of the year.

Stop at Laugarvatn, where steam emerges at the edge of a lake, forming a natural sauna. Optional swim in the lake! Head back to Reykjavik and listen to a few sagas on the way. Dinner in the Evening.

Monday: Return to London.

Listening Extract 16

Eastern Travel is a Cairo-based company that supplies packages to European tour operators. Listen to three employees finalize details of a cruise on the River Nile and complete the itinerary.

Exploring the Nile Valley

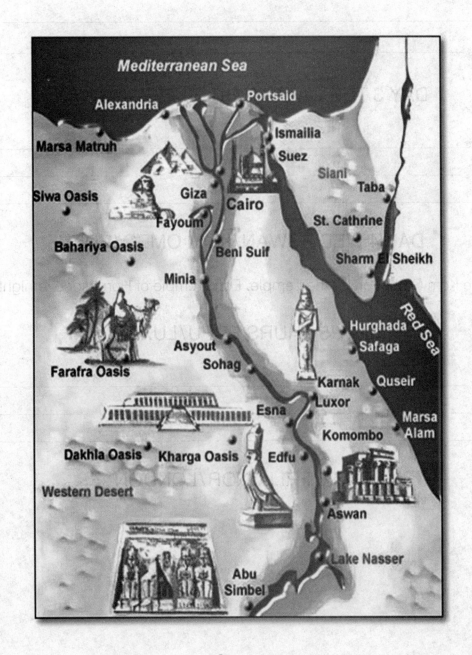

DAY 1 SUN LONDON/CAIRO

Depart from Heathrow on an Egyptair flight to Cairo. Stay at the Le Meridien Pyramids Hotel.

DAY 2 MON CAIRO

1. _____
2. _____

DAY 3 TUE CAIRO/ABU SIMBEL/ASWAN

3. _____
4. _____
5. _____

DAY 4 WED ASWAN/KOM OMBO/EDFU

Arrive Kom Ombo to visit the Temple. Edfu Temple of Horus for overnight stay.

DAY 5 THURS EDFU/LUXOR

6. _____
7. _____
8. _____

DAY 6 FRI LUXOR/LONDON

Listening Transcript for Extract 16

(Courtesy of Strutt, English for International Tourism Intermediate Students' Book, Unit 12, Exercise 13: 143–144)

Chairperson	OK, let's get this meeting started. Has everyone got the draft itinerary?
All	Yes.
Chairperson	Good, so what we have to do is complete the missing days and if we can finish this today then we'll be in a position to offer it to Kuoni for their catalogue. So, as I understand it they will be taking people out on a scheduled flight and putting them up in the Meridian Pyramids Hotel for two nights. What we need to look at this is the sightseeing part of the holiday.
Orla	So, what about Day 2? I guess the pyramids at Giza are the obvious choice.
Imad	That sounds like a good idea to begin with but we could do that as a half-day excursion and then do the Egyptian Museum and the Tutankhamun collection in the afternoon.
Orla	That might be possible but it's a lot for one day. I'm not sure about that.
Chairperson	Well, if we use a good guide who just shows them the most essential things then they only need spend a couple of hours at the museum. That's probably enough for most people.
Orla	OK. It might be possible. But wouldn't it be better if the pyramid tour and the museum were pre-booked?
Imad	You're right. I think it would be better.
Orla	Fine.
Chairperson	Right. Day 3. There's a bit of a problem here because you actually have to get up at two in the morning for the six o'clock Egyptair flight to Abu Simbel. But I don't think we need to say that you have to get up early.
Orla	No, Neither do I. It would put people off going on the trip.
Chairperson	So they arrive in Abu Simbel and then they get on the coach and go

	off to the temple of Ramses II and after that the Temple of Hathor. That's actually quite a short visit so they could have a felucca ride in the afternoon.
Orla	That's a nice idea but I think it'd be more interesting for them if we flew them to the Aswan Dam.
Imad	That's a good idea. And they could stay on board ship and sail overnight to Kom Ombo, couldn't they?
Chairperson	It'd be more expensive but it sounds great. Let's put "overnight on board Aswan". OK. And then on Day 4 they arrive in Kom Ombo. They can visit the temple and then get back on board and sail on to Edfu.
Imad	Right. So after visiting the Temple of Horus at Edfu they can continue on board overnight to Luxor, arriving early Thursday.
Chairperson	That's great. So for Wednesday we can put the Temple of Kom Ombo, then the Temple of Horus at Edfu and finally on board overnight Edfu.
Imad	And when they arrive in Luxor Thursday morning, how about a visit to Valley of the Kings and Queens, followed by the Temple of Queen Hatshepsut, which leaves the afternoon to relax before the flight back?
Chairperson	What do you think?
Orla	That's fine. And what about offering an optional extra few days in Luxor with excursions to the Karnak complex?
Imad	OK. But we'll have to work out a separate price for that.
Chairperson	Definitely!

Listening Extract 17

Tour operators, airlines and national tourist boards often run "educationals" (also called "familiarization trips") for people in the travel trade who are in a position to promote a particular destination. Listen to Helen Lee describing a familiarization trip to China and follow the itinerary on the map. Then listen again and complete the following itinerary worksheet.

China Familiarization Trip

	Places	Attractions
1	London/Beijing (3 nights)	1.1 1.2 1.3
2	Beijing/_____ _____/Beijing	2.1 2.2 2.3
3	Beijing/_____ (1 night)	
4	_____/Shanghai (1 night)	4.1 4.2 4.3
5	Shanghai/_____ _____/Shanghai (1 night)	5.1 5.2
6	Shanghai/_____ _____/Guilin	6.1 6.2 6.3
7	_____/Hong Kong (Cathay Pacific)	

Listening Transcript for Extract 17

(Courtesy of Jacob & Strutt, English for International Tourism Post-Intermediate Students' Book, Unit 7, Listening 2: 119)

Helen Good Morning everyone. My name's Helen Lee and I'm going to describe the itinerary to you and tell you a little bit about what you'll be seeing. It's a fifteen-day tour which covers the main tourist spots and also goes down to HongKong as well, so it gives you a good introduction to China if you've never been there before.

Easter's quite a good time to go; the weather's getting a bit warmer than in the north of China. It'll be quite pleasant in the south... but really the best times to go are May to June and then in the autumn, but obviously they're the times when there are going to be more people around. But we start our tours going just before Easter.

You'll be flying London to Beijing to start with and staying for three nights and doing the most famous places like the Forbidden City where the emperors used to live, the Summer Palace up in the west of the city, the Temple of Heaven, and just time to stroll around, have a look at the streets, go shopping, and so on.

You'll have the experience of two guides with you, a national guide who'll stay with you all the way through the tour and a local Chinese guide — both trained English speaking guides, so you'll have the benefit of their knowledge.

And then from Beijing we go by coach to a smaller city in the north called Chengde which is — or rather was — the summer resort of the emperors and there's a pretty park there and we visit three temples. One of them is very reminiscent of the Potola Palace in Lhasa. And on the way there we stop at a certain part of the Wall called Jin shan Ling and have a picnic on the Wall — It's slightly quieter than the other places on the Wall which tend to be packed with tourists, so this is nicer.

And then from Chengde we go back to Beijing and then connect with a flight to Xi'an which is the beginning of the Silk Road and is famous for the Terracotta Warriors that everybody's heard about, and we (will have) lunch at the Warriors and go on to the Banpo Neolithic Village, the Huaqing Hot Springs and other sightseeing spots.

Then we go down to Shanghai for one night, and a couple of hours on a train to Suzhou which is known as the Venice of the East because it's a canal city and it's where a third of the silk is actually produced in China, so it's quite an interesting place. And it's famous for its gardens so we go there too to see the gardens. And there'll be a visit to a silk factory as well.

And then go back to Shanghai, another night there, and the following day go down to Guilin which is a very well-known city — more in the countryside than other places you'll be visiting... for its river, the Lijiang River, and its magnificent limestone formations along the river bank. So there'll be a river trip all the way down to the small town of Yangshuo where there's an interesting market which sells wild animals, flowers and plants and herbal medicines, and then back up to Guilin afterwards. There's also an optional excursion you can take in the evening to see cormorant fishermen at work — they have rafts and they have their own private cormorant and the birds dive down and bring the fish up to the surface and it's quite fascinating to see that.

OK, are there any questions so far?

Travel Agent Yes, when do we get to go to Hong Kong?

Helen Well, we're flying there the following day — it only takes an hour. Your guide will actually leave you in Guilin, and in Hong Kong you're basically left to do your own thing — there's no sightseeing included. You'll be staying at the Metropole Hotel which belongs to our group and you can book onto tours there. And then the final day, we fly by Cathay Pacific. So, by the end of the tour, hopefully you'll have learnt a lot about China.

Listening Extract 18

18.1 Melanie is a resort representative for Inghams, a UK tour operator. Listen to her describe the holiday entertainment and complete the program.

```
                    PROGRAM OF EVENTS

                Morning           Afternoon              Evening
Sunday          _____        _____             (1) Welcome meeting
Monday Ski School                 (2) _____         _____
Tuesday (3) _____            Children's race
Wednesday Ski School              (4) _____         _____
Thursday Ski School               Beginner's race        (5) _____
Friday Ski School                 _____             (6) _____

Events and times are subject to change.
```

Guidelines to Itinerary Design

1. Convenience & feasibility
2. For pleasure not for hardship
3. Delete, supplement or adapt as appropriate
4. Adequate free time
5. Diversified arrangements

18.2 Listen again and answer the questions.

1. Where is the welcome meeting?

2. On what condition can children go cross-country skiing?

3. What is "snowshoeing"?

4. Where is the demonstration of new ski equipment?

5. Who can take part in the torchlit descent of the mountain?

6. What is organized for the farewell party?

7. Where should people sign up for the activities?

Itinerary Negotiation Focus

1. *Catering*   2. *Lodging*   3. *Transportation*
4. *Sightseeing*   5. *Shopping*   6. *Entertainment*

What is familiarization trip?

A familiarization trip is often run by tour operators, airlines and national tourist boards for people in the travel trade who are in a position to promote a particular destination.

Listening Transcript for Extract 18

(Courtesy of Dubicka & O'Keeffe, English for International Tourism Pre-intermediate Students' Book, Unit 12, Exercise 15–16: 141)

Good afternoon everybody. If I could just have your attention for one moment, I have some information for you about the activities we've organized for you this week with Inghams.

Thank you. We've lots of entertainments in store for you, starting this evening at half past eight with the welcome meeting in the hotel lounge.

You'll be delighted to know that includes a free drink.

Now, tomorrow morning the ski school starts and then in the afternoon I'm leading a group cross-country skiing. Children aged twelve and over can come along, but they must be accompanied by an adult.

On Tuesday morning we'll be snowshoeing. In case you're not sure what that is, it's basically trekking in the snow wearing things that look like tennis rackets on your feet. But seriously, you don't have to be a skier to take part, we'll organize the hire equipment and it's lots of fun.

Now where was I? Oh yes, on Wednesday afternoon there's a demonstration of some fantastic new ski equipment in the hotel lobby.

Thursday evening at six o'clock there's a torchlit descent of the mountain. All you advanced skiers can participate in that if you want. We'll provide the transport from the hotel at 6:00 p.m.

On Friday night we have our farewell party which with a live band, dancing and there'll also be a karaoke competition. We'll also be organizing lots of races and competitions throughout the week on the slopes and we're offering lots of super prizes.

You can sign up for the activities on the notice-board in the hotel lobby and you can talk to me if you need any help or advice. I hope you all have a fantastic time this week with Inghams.

Culture Interpretation 6 Folklores and Legendary Figures

Vocabulary Workshop

Are you familiar with the following expressions in the Chinese culture? Please discuss with your group members about their stories.

1. 盘古开天	2. 伏羲八卦	3. 女娲补天	4. 精卫填海	5. 共工怒触不周山
6. 祝融火神	7. 神农尝百草	8. 夸父逐日	9. 后羿射日	10. 嫦娥奔月
11. 仓颉造字	12. 大禹治水	13. 愚公移山	14. 炎黄子孙	15. 玉皇大帝
16. 瑶池王母	17. 牛郎织女	18. 八仙过海	19. 麻姑献寿	20. 刘海戏金蟾
21. 和合二仙	22. 钟馗嫁妹	23. 五子登科	24. 哪吒闹海	25. 福禄寿三星
26. 高山流水	27. 西施浣纱	28. 昭君出塞	29. 貂蝉拜月	30. 贵妃醉酒
31. 门神	32. 妈祖	33. 龙王	34. 哼哈二将	35. 四大天王
36. 弥勒/韦陀	37. 观音菩萨	38. 释迦/如来	39. 文殊/普贤	40. 地藏王
41. 罗汉	42. 飞天	43. 济公	44. 孙悟空	45. 猪八戒
46. 沙和尚	47. 唐僧师徒	48. 孔子	49. 鲁班	50. 华佗
51. 关羽	52. 包拯	53. 诸葛亮	54. 岳飞	55. 郑和
56. 八卦	57. 儒家思想	58. 道家思想	59. 佛教	60. 暗八仙

Group Project

Suppose you are going to design a set of PPT slides for an International Tour Culture Festival. In an event, you are asked to nominate 20 legendary figures representing the most five remarkable aspects in the Chinese culture (e. g. courage, benevolence, righteousness, loyalty, wisdom, passion, tolerance, goodwill, faith, courtesy, humor, fortune, friendship, sympathy, brotherhood, kindness, etc.). For each aspect, please recommend 4 candidates and demonstrate your reasons. Please prepare your project in the following procedure.

1. Discuss what five aspects of the Chinese culture you are going to display to the international tourists.
2. Decide who will be the 20 candidates in your presentation.
3. Find five reasons for each candidate.
4. Share your preparation work among your group members.
5. Produce your PPT slides individually.
6. Put your slides together and arrange them in good order.
7. Print out your PPT slides in the handout format (every 6 slides in one page) and hand it in on the day of presentation.
8. Please refer to the following worksheet to initiate your project work discussion.

Cultural Symbol	Candidates	Reasons
1.	1.	1.
		2.
		3.
		4.
		5.

Assignment 6 Role-play Tasks

Scenario 6 - A

Ms. Maria Leech and Mr. Nick Patterson are both Summer China-study Tour Program Officers of West Pacific College, Canada. They come to your company as invited to take a familiarization trip in China. Please design an itinerary for them.

Scenario 6 - B

As your company is responsible for providing a local guide for their 3-day travel in Beijing, a detailed local itinerary in Beijing needs to be presented in the meeting. Please discuss with your group members and produce it to your clients.

Scenario 6 - C

For Ms. Maria Leech and Mr. Nick Patterson, you need to confirm the following details in the report meeting to your Chinese colleagues.
   1. The guide service.
   2. The connecting transportation and the local transportation.
   3. The conditions of accommodation and lodging.
   4. Adequate free time or arrangement for shopping and entertainment.
   5. Other suggestions related to the itineraries.

Scenario 6 - D

Warm - up Reading for Scenario D

Forward: The following Chinese itinerary was designed by a client Miss Wang who made this after consulting her own travel books. This itinerary was designed for Miss Wang's cousin, Miss Woo No-mei（吴诺美）, a 21 year-old Chinese-French student, who plans to travel to China this summer together with a German, a French and a Japanese classmate. Miss Wu can only understand Wenzhou Dialect. She can also speak very little Putonghua but can't read Chinese at all.

第一天：下午飞机抵首都机场；住市中心某单位内部招待所。土府井逛街、胡同游、北京小吃，晚上参观国家博物馆、首都博物馆。

第二天：看升旗，参观清华、北大、动物园，在北大食堂用餐，天坛、雍和宫、先农坛、地坛、月坛、日坛。

第三天：颐和园、香山、长城、周口店、恭王府、前门、琉璃厂、鲁迅故居、抗战纪念馆、卢沟桥、国子监、郭守敬纪念馆、徐悲鸿纪念馆、毛主席故居、周总理故居、饺子馆、老北京炸酱面。

第四天：十三陵、孔庙、天安门、北海、故宫、东来顺涮肉、北京烤鸭、老城一锅羊蝎子、看降旗。

第五天：景山、工艺美术馆、国家美术馆、国家图书馆、少年儿童图书馆、麻辣诱惑、郭林家常菜、贵州人酒家、看京剧、杂技、郭德纲相声、赵本山小品。

第六天：中国科技馆、自然博物馆、天文馆、人民大会堂、毛主席纪念堂、国务院、什刹海酒吧街、三里屯酒吧街、簋街、西单购物，晚上坐火车去丽江。

北京（6天）— 火车往丽江（2天）— 火车往苏州（2天）— 火车往开封（2天）— 火车往洛阳（2天）— 飞机往上海（2天）— 坐船往杭州（1天）— 火车往西安（3天）— 飞机回法国

Please role-play the following scenarios in English with your group members.

Scenario 6 - D - 1

When Miss Wang comes to your agency, an agent is just on duty. He/she receives her and explains what has been changed in the English itinerary to her.

Scenario 6 - D - 2

Miss Wang then tells her cousin about the changes by telephone. But she still can't explain why it has been changed like that when her cousin asks her some detailed things. Then Miss Wu tells her German, French, and Japanese friends about the changes. They also have some questions about the itinerary which Miss Wu can't give satisfactory answers.

Scenario 6 - D - 3

When they come to China, Miss Wang brings the four people to the agency again and asks the agents to answer their questions about the itinerary. Fortunately, there are Chinese-English, (German-English, French-English, Spanish-English, Russia-English, Japanese-English) translators in this agency and with their joint efforts the communications go on very smoothly.

Scenario – D – 1

Scenario – D – 2

Scenario – D – 3

Unit 7

Scenario Warm-up 7 Guiding Speech 1

Culture Interpretation 7 Traditional Festivals

Assignment 7 Pair Intrepretation Tasks

Scenario Warm-up 7 Guiding Speech 1

Listening Extract 19

Jenny is a bus tour guide in Barcelona. Listen and tick the difficulties she has.

(   ) 1. The tourists asked her a lot of questions.
(   ) 2. She forgot or didn't know some of the information.
(   ) 3. One of the tourists didn't hear her.
(   ) 4. The tourists didn't want to pay for the fountain show.
(   ) 5. A thief stole a woman's handbag.
(   ) 6. A child wanted to go swimming in the fountains.

Listening Transcript for Extract 19

(Courtesy of Dubicka & O'Keeffe, English for International Tourism Pre-intermediate Students' Book, Unit 4, Exercise 12: 134)

Jenny	And on your left you can see the sculpture, Woman and Bird by the famous Catalan artist, Joan Miró.
Tourist A	It doesn't look like a woman to me, dad.
Tourist B	Sssh!
Jenny	Now our next stop in Barcelona is the famous Magic Fountains in Plaça d'Espanya. The fountains were built in er, um... quite a long time ago. This show of beautiful colored fountains first started at the time of the Olympic Games, in 1992. Maybe you saw them on television. Do you remember the song Barcelona by Freddie Mercury and the well-known opera singer, Montserrat Caballé? And now you can see the Magic Fountains most evenings in the summer. There's a show every half hour.
Tourist C	What time does the next show start?
Jenny	Let me see. There's one starting in five minutes, at 9:30 p.m.
Tourist C	And how long does it take?
Jenny	About half an hour. Please be back at the bus by 10:15 p.m.
Tourist D	Excuse me, did you say the Olympic stadium was near here?
Jenny	That's right, the sports stadium we visited this afternoon is further up the hill. This area is known as Montjuïc. You can see the fountains now straight ahead. Please be careful of pickpockets and look after your money and valuables.
Tourist C	Excuse me, what did she say?
Tourist B	Pickpockets — people who steal your money. So look after your bag.
Tourist C	Oh, I see. Thank you. And how much does it cost to see the fountains?
Jenny	Nothing, it's free.
Tourist A	Hey, dad, can we swim in the fountains?
Tourist B	No, you can't swim in the fountains.

Jenny   Here we are. No swimming is allowed in the fountains but if you'd like some refreshments or a drink, there's a café over there. This is the last stop on our tour today, so please be ready by a quarter past ten so we can be back at the hotel on time. Thank you.

Listening Extract 20

Listen to the guide talk about the Natural History Museum in London and complete the extract with the words and phrases she uses.

OK everybody? We're now standing outside the main entrance to the Natural History Museum, which is one of the finest examples of London's __1__ architecture. The building was designed by the architect Alfred Waterhouse using an iron and __2__ framework hidden behind arches and columns which if you look closely, are decorated with sculptures of __3__ and plants. The museum houses a whole host of exhibits of __4__ and mammals, as well as insects and plants. There are also __5__ devoted to human biology and the origin of species. You can also visit the __6__ where you can find out what it's like to be in the middle of an earthquake or standing next to a volcano. Entrance to the museum is __7__ and there's a __8__ a bookshop and a gift shop if you get hungry or want to buy any souvenirs.

7-step Guiding Speech Writing Tips

Step 1   Introduce the site: *First of all, we're going to visit... We are now...*

Step 2   Say what its main features are: *The palace is the home of... The museum/gallery... it was built in (date)...*

Step 3   Mention other attractions/benefits: *You can also see... There's a...*

Step 4   Mention possible restrictions: *Please note that photography is not allowed.*

Step 5   Give information about times and prices: *The museum closes at (time)... Entrance to the museum... costs...*

Step 6   Invite questions: *Does anyone have any questions?*

Step 7   Be enthusiastic and use positive language: *It's ... examples of 19th century architecture.*

Listening Transcript for Extract 20

(Courtesy of Strutt, English for International Tourism Intermediate Students' Book, Unit 8, Exercise 20: 138)

OK everybody? We're now standing outside the main entrance to the Natural History Museum, which is one of the best examples of London's 19th century architecture. As you can see, the building looks very much like a cathedral and was designed by the architect Alfred Waterhouse using an iron and steel framework hidden behind arches and columns, which, if you look closely, are decorated with sculptures of animals and plants.

The museum houses a whole host of exhibits of dinosaurs, mammals, as well as insects and plants. There are also displays devoted to human biology and the origin of species.

You can also visit the Earth galleries where you can find out what it's like to be in the middle of an earthquake or standing next to a volcano.

Entrance to the museum is free and there's a cafeteria if you get hungry, and a bookshop and a gift shop if you want to buy any souvenirs.

Listening Extract 21

A tourist follows a tour of Wawel Hill. Listen and match the events with the dates and periods you hear.

1. Vistulan people inhabited Wawel Hill
2. Tho Castle and Cathedral were built
3. Warsaw became the capital of Poland
4. Wawel Castle suffered from political conflicts
5. Wawel Castle was restored

(a) in the 20th century.
(b) in the 17th and 18th centuries.
(c) in ancient times.
(d) at the beginning of the 17th century.
(e) in the late medieval period.

Listening Transcript for Extract 21

(Courtesy of Dubicka & O'Keeffe, English for International Tourism Pre-intermediate Students' Book, Unit 10, Exercise 11: 139)

Guide Hello — excuse me — thank you. If I may have your attention please... Thank you. Before we begin the tour, I'd like to give you a brief history of the castle. Wawel Hill was first inhabited by the Vistulan people in ancient times. Later, in the late mediaeval period, from the fourteenth century the royal residence and a new cathedral were built. But it was the kings of the Jagiellonian dynasty who turned this Gothic castle into one of the most magnificent Renaissance castles in Central Europe.

Tourist Wasn't Cracow the capital of Poland?

Guide That's correct. Although Warsaw became the capital at the beginning of the seventeenth century, royal coronations continued to take place in Cracow and it remained a centre of historical and cultural importance.

Tourist Wasn't it destroyed in the wars?

Guide Well, not exactly. In the seventeenth and eighteenth centuries the castle suffered from political conflicts, but an intensive restoration program in the twentieth century saved the castle and cathedral. Fortunately, Wawel also escaped destruction in both world wars. Right, now let's turn to the statue of Tadeusz Kościuszko just in front of us. He was the general who was responsible for the insurrection of 1794 against the Russian army...

Culture Interpretation 7 Traditional Festivals

Vocabulary Workshop

Are you familiar with the following festivals and customs? Share your ideas with your group members. Please translate the following words into English.

1. 腊八	2. 除夕	3. 春节	4. 元宵节	5. 清明节
6. 端午节	7. 中秋节	8. 七夕	9. 重阳节	10. 除尘
11. 祭灶	12. 门神	13. 春联	14. 灯笼	15. 包饺子
16. 爆竹	17. 焰火	18. 红包	19. 舞狮	20. 舞龙
21. 秧歌	22. 旱船	23. 高跷	24. 花车	25. 舞中幡
26. 杂技	27. 魔术	28. 腰鼓	29. 武术	30. 盛装游行
31. 木偶戏	32. 皮影戏	33. 灯会	34. 花会	35. 庙会
36. 进香	37. 祭祖	38. 踏青	39. 荡秋千	40. 放风筝
41. 寒食	42. 放河灯	43. 会船	44. 赛龙舟	45. 包粽子
46. 吃月饼	47. 赏月	48. 登高	49. 赏菊	50. 家宴
51. 复活节	52. 母亲节	53. 感恩节	54. 圣诞节	55. 情人节
56. 劳动节	57. 青年节	58. 儿童节	59. 妇女节	60. 国庆节

Group Project

Please design a Chinese Festival Tour Itinerary brochure with your group members for the international tourists in Beijing. You need to prepare a 15-20 minutes' PPT presentation to display your findings, creations, imaginations and suggestions. The following procedure may be used as a reference. Please discuss what programs may appeal to the international tourists, and fill in the event brainstorm worksheet below.

Festivals	What to do?	When & Where?
Spring Festival	Day 1	
Lantern Festival	Event 1	
Qing Ming Festival		
Dragon Boat Festival	Event 2	
Mid-autumn Festival		
Double Ninth Festival	Event 3	
	Day 2	
	Event 4	
	Event 5	
	Event 6	
	Day 3	
	Event 7	
	Event 8	

Assignment 7 Pair Interpretation Tasks

7-A 中国饮食文化

　　中国菜主要有四大菜系，分别是川菜、鲁菜、粤菜和淮扬菜。传统的上菜程序可分为以下八个步骤：一、茶水/饮料；二、小菜；三、凉菜；四、辅菜；五、主菜；六、汤；七、米饭/点心；八、水果。美食家主要从色、香、味三个角度去鉴赏菜肴的质量。中国菜的口味非常丰富，酸、甜、苦、辣、咸各种口味都有代表菜。中国菜的烹饪工艺也比较复杂，主要由选料、刀工、调味、入味和火候几个方面构成。火锅是中餐中一个独特的菜类，传统的中式火锅分为蒙式和川式两大类。除了西餐中常见的盘子外，碗和筷子也是中餐的特色餐具。

7-B 中国十二生肖

　　和西方的12星座类似，中国也有12生肖动物。但是星座代表的大致是1年的时间，中国生肖代表12个年份。这种纪年法我们用了几千年了，十二生肖对应的12个动物分别是鼠、牛、虎、兔、龙、蛇、马、羊、猴、鸡、狗、猪。比如说我，生于1976年，我的生肖是龙。大家可以推算自己的生肖，以后在纪念品商店您会发现很多东西都和生肖有关。当然了，和西方星象学类似，中国古代也有算命先生，为无知的人们推算命运。中国传统上也有哪些生肖的人适合结婚的说法。但是在现代社会，随着科学观念的普及，很多人早已不相信这些迷信、非理性的说法了。

7-C 中国书画艺术

　　中国的书法和绘画是最能体现中国文人精神的艺术形式。在古代中国，虽然现代科学技术并没有很早地来到人们的生活中，但这个古老的东方国度，并不是愚昧无知的蛮荒之地，而是充满诗情画意的文化圣地。两千年以前，当中国不幸从一个统一的国家分裂成数个弱小的诸侯国时，中国的书法、绘画和散文艺术就开始走向巅峰。再后来无论国家统一还是分裂，这种对艺术的热爱从来没有减弱；到了一千多年前，中国的社会又几乎成为了诗人的海洋；五百年前，也就是莎士比亚生活的时代，中国的戏剧创作同样走到了第一个巅峰。无论是快乐还是苦闷，中国的文人总愿意把感情融入书画的每一个笔触之间。有意思的是，中国古代出名的画家很多都不是职业书画家，有很多著名的诗人、画家、书法家甚至就是皇帝。在中国古代教育中，写诗和画画往往是孩子成长教育中必修的部分。由此不难看出，中国人很早就形成了发达的东方审美体系。

Unit 8

Scenario Warm-up 8 Guiding Speech 2

Culture Interpretation 8 Traditional Costumes & Chinese Operas

Assignment 8 Pair Interpretation Tasks

Scenario Warm-up 8 Guiding Speech 2

Listening Extract 22

Noh, Kabuki and Bunraku are three forms of traditional Japanese theater. Listen to a tour guide in the lobby of the Kabuki-za Theater in Tokyo and complete the table below.

Type	Origins	Audience	Themes	Costume	Stage	Music
Noh						
Kabuki						
Bunraku						

Listening Transcript for Extract 22

(Courtesy of Strutt, English for International Tourism Intermediate Students' Book, Unit 11, Exercise 12: 141-142)

Before we go in to see the performance I would like to tell you something about Japanese traditional theater. There are three major types of traditional theater performed in Japan. There are Noh, Kabuki and Bunraku.

Noh is a very old form of theater dating back to the 14th century and was enjoyed by the higher social classes. The plays tell stories about gods, warriors, beautiful women and supernatural beings. The leading characters wear masks and speak and sing in a very monotonous way, accompanied by a chorus and musicians playing traditional drums and flutes. The wooden stage is usually outdoors and has a roof supported by four columns and there's just a single pine tree as scenery.

Noh theater is very slow and dramatic but kabuki is much more colorful and has a large cast. The origins go back to the 17th century and kabuki was the popular culture of ordinary people. The plays are often about historical events and relationships between men and women. In the early years, both men and women acted in Kabuki plays but later women were not allowed and so all actors are now men. Unlike Noh theater, in Kabuki no one wears a mask but the make-up is very elaborate and exaggerated.

The stage is also different and is equipped with several gadgets like revolving sets and trapdoors through which the actors can appear and disappear. Another specialty of the kabuki stage is a footbridge, the hanamichi, that leads through the audience and is used for dramatic entrance and exits.

Bunraku is traditional Japanese puppet theater that has its origin in the Edo Period, that is from the early 17th century up until about 1850. The content of Bunraku and Kabuki plays is very similar and often deals with emotional conflict, like when two lovers choose to commit suicide.

The puppets are about one point two meters tall and are manipulated by three people, the puppeteer who wears traditional formal dress and the two assistants who are both in black. Each person is responsible for a different part of the puppet. There's also traditional music that's performed on an instrument called a shamisen which is a kind of guitar with three strings.

Okay. So we are now going to go into the Kabuki-za but first of all you should collect your headphones so that you can follow the action in English.

Listening Extract 23

Listen to the short presentation on Moscow and pay attention to the information under these headings: climate, getting around, sightseeing, entertainment, food & drink. Have you got any idea about how to deliver a city profile guiding speech?

Climate	Getting Around	Sightseeing	Food & Drink	Entertainment
Seasons	Metro	Museums	Restaurants	Shows
Temperature	Bus	Monuments	Takeaways	Festivals
Rainfall	Train	Parks	Local Specialties	Nightclubs

Based on the format above, please write down some basic facts about Beijing. Then compare your writing with your partners.

Climate	Getting Around	Sightseeing	Food & Drink	Entertainment
Seasons	Metro	Museums	Restaurants	Shows
Temperature	Bus	Monuments	Takeaways	Festivals
Rainfall	Train	Parks	Local Specialties	Nightclubs

Listening Transcript for Extract 23

(Courtesy of Strutt, English for International Tourism Intermediate Students' Book, Unit 2, Exercise 14: 131)

The best time to go to Moscow is July and August because they are the warmest months of the year. Summer days are long and it can rain quite a lot. By the end of November Moscow is frozen most of the time and snow stays until April.

Getting around is easy and relatively cheap. You can get between all five airports and the city center by a combination of bus and metro or suburban train. It's a good idea to book a transfer, which means you'll be picked up and driven to your hotel for little more than the cost of a taxi.

Most visitors to Moscow come to see the Kremlin, Red Square and St Basil's Cathedral and to look at Lenin's Tomb and it's best to see the central area around the Kremlin on foot. For other parts of the city, the fastest, cheapest and easiest way to get around is on the metro. There are more than 150 metro stations — some of them with amazing architecture — and you don't have to wait long for a train. Buses, trolleybuses and trams run almost everywhere the metro doesn't go. The most famous of Moscow's parks and gardens is Gorky Park which stretches almost three kilometers along the river Moskva. There's a fairground, an ornamental garden and in summer boats leave from the pier on river excursions.

There are a number of festivals that are worth seeing. The Moscow Film Festival takes place in the autumn and the Russian Winter Festival is a must, with troyka rides, folklore shows, games and vodka. The live music scene is good, with regular gigs at numerous venues. As far as eating out is concerned, for an authentic Russian experience go to Petrovich where the walls are covered by all sorts of reminders of the Soviet past. For a quick snack, there are three chains of food stalls — Niam Niam, which sells all kind of sweet and savory pies, Kroshka Kartoshka, which are jacket potatoes with filings and Russkie Bliny, which of course needs no explanation.

Culture Interpretation 8 Traditional Costumes & Chinese Operas

Vocabulary Workshop

Have you seen the Chinese traditional costumes? If yes, in what occasions? Please translate the following words into English and identify for what role or in what occasion they are allowed to wear in Chinese opera?

1. 冠	2. 帽	3. 盔	4. 巾	5. 袍
6. 平天冠	7. 凤冠	8. 紫金冠	9. 王帽	10. 罗帽
11. 乌纱	12. 夫子盔	13. 蝴蝶盔	14. 钻天盔	15. 帅盔
16. 文生巾	17. 道巾	18. 夫子巾	19. 员外巾	20. 观音兜
21. 月牙箍	22. 翎子	23. 虎头靴	24. 高方靴	25. 靠
26. 护心镜	27. 靠旗	28. 蟒袍	29. 玉带	30. 官衣
31. 补子	32. 宫衣	33. 氅	34. 褶子	35. 帔
36. 箭衣	37. 饭兜	38. 云肩	39. 坎肩	40. 道袍
41. 法衣	42. 袈裟	43. 斗篷	44. 花脸	45. 髯口
46. 头面	47. 旗袍	48. 旗头	49. 日式和服	50. 中山装
51. 唐装	52. 上衣下裳	53. 交领右衽	54. 钟袖博带	55. 曲裾

Do you know how to wear a Chinese opera costume and what dressing procedure is involved?

These are the pictures of a well-dressed girl in Chinese traditional costume. Can you think of how many steps involved in putting on the beautiful spiral dress? Then please match the following mixed pictures in the right order.

Jigsaw Game: How to Dress Spiral Dress

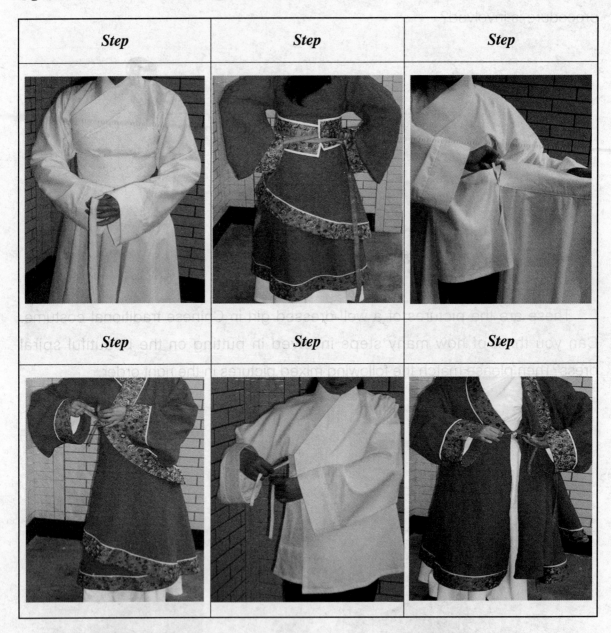

Step 1 *Tying the ribbons of upper suit like that in bath robe*

Step 2 *Wearing upper first, under later*

Step 3 *Putting on the outer dress*

Step 4 *Wrapping the lower hem*

Step 5 *Tying it with the collar ribbon*

Step 6 *Tying the belt at back*

Do you know how to make up in Chinese opera?

Can you believe a beautiful girl can be played by a totally different-looking man through magic Chinese Opera make-up?

经化妆师马玉秋重塑的《荀慧生》男旦艺术形象　　京剧表演艺术家荀慧生先生（1900—1968）

Then please match the following mixed pictures in the correct order.

Jigsaw Game: Make-up Procedure of Chinese Opera Lady Role

Step	Step	Step

Step	Step	Step

Step 1 *Fastening the head with belt*（勒头）

Step 2 *Sticking the artificial tress*（贴片子）

Step 3 *Fastening the wig with wires*（绑假发）

Step 4 *Sticking the bun and pigtail*（梳木头）

Step 5 *Wearing the hairpins & jewelry*（带头面）

Step 6 *Make a debut pose*（定妆亮相）

Group Project A

Suppose you are going to design an advertisement leaflet for a Chinese Traditional Costume Photo Studio in a City Temple Fair. Please prepare your project in the following procedure.

1. Discuss with your group about what costume should be chosen for the photo studio and decide 10 sets of them in terms of the role's age, gender, career, social class, character, etc.
2. Find a suitable background for the costume show and write a profile to describe your design.
3. Share your preparation work among your group members.
4. Produce your PPT slides individually.
5. Put your slides together and arrange them in good order.
6. Print out your PPT slides in the handout format (every 6 slides in one page) and hand it in on the day of presentation.

The following worksheet may be helpful to your project work.

Costume Type	Role Stereotype	Background Scene
Head Gear	Age	Site
Coat	Gender	Settings
Shoes	Career or Social Class	Props

Translafion Workshop

Are you familiar with Chinese operas? Please translate the following operas into English? Have you ever seen the Chinese operas stated below? Tell them to your classmates. If not, please give an example that you are familiar with.

Chinese Names	English Names	Representative Arias, Duets, or Stunts Shows
1. 京剧		《四郎探母——坐宫》 《三岔口》 《贵妃醉酒》
2. 昆曲		《牡丹亭——春香闹学》
3. 越剧		《梁山伯与祝英台——十八相送》
4. 黄梅戏		《天仙配——夫妻双双把家还》
5. 豫剧		《花木兰——谁说女子不如男》
6. 评剧		《花为媒——报花名》
7. 川剧		《变脸》
8. 绍剧		《猴戏》

Group Project B

1. Please discuss with your group members and try to find 3 famous lyrics from Chinese operas that you think can best represent the Chinese culture.

2. Please design a repertoire for a 30-45 minutes' Chinese opera show and search for the audio or video clips from the Internet sources.

3. Then please write synopsis, e. g. the background story, roles, how to identify them by costumes as well as the plot, for each program.

4. Please try to translate all the Chinese lyrics into English.

5. Put all you have prepared in good order in just one PPT file.

6. Share your presentation work and demonstrate it in front of your classmates.

越剧选段《张羽煮海——听琴》	
疏剌剌恰似晚风落万松, 响潺潺分明是流水绝涧中。 这分明是我私谱的"鱼龙曲", 却为何竟在这仙客指下弄? 适才我琴思忽断曲未终, 她竟然信手续来天衣无缝。 我只道子期一去赏音孤, 难道说高山流水今相逢?	

京剧选段《三家店——秦琼发配》　　Farewell Friends, Farewell Mom!

将身儿来至在大街口，	Walking on the street
尊一声过往的宾朋听从头。	Listening to my story from begin
一不是响马并贼寇，	I'm not the robber, nor the thief
二不是歹人把城偷。	Nor am I the hoodlum grabbing the poor
杨林与我来争斗，	Cause Yang Lin conflicting with me
因此上发配到登州。	That's why here am I
舍不得太爷的恩情厚，	Can't forget the lord's protection
舍不得衙役们众班头。	Can't forget the brothers with whom I work at court
实难舍街坊四邻与我的好朋友，	Oh! Farewell my neighbors, my friends
舍不得老娘亲白了头。	How can I forget mom in hair white
娘生儿连心肉，	To mom, I'm her flesh of heart
儿行千里母担忧。	To mom, each my step making her heartbeat
儿想娘亲难叩首，	Even a thousand miles away
娘想儿来泪双流。	Oh, mom, I can never kowtow to you
眼见得红日坠落在西山后，	Oh, mom, I can see your tears dripping like streams
叫一声解差把店投。	I can see red sun's falling down behind the mountain's back
	Oh, come on my guard! Let's go to the inn for a rest

越剧选段《何文秀——桑园访妻》　Mulberry Orchard Visit

路遇大姐得音讯　九里桑园访兰英	Thanking for the lady's help
行过三里桃花渡　走过六里杏花村	Let me go to the mulberry orchard to see my darling
七宝凉亭来穿过　九里桑园面前呈	Passing 3 miles' Peach Flower Ferry
但只见一座桑园多茂盛	And the 6 miles' Apricot Flower Village
眼看人家十数份	With 7 pavilions flying in my eyes
那一边竹篱茅舍围得深	Here's the nine-mile-away mulberry orchard
莫非就是杨家门	Bushy, leafy are the trees
待我上前把门推	Dozen cottages scattering around
为什么青天白日门关紧	Where's my darling's house
耳听内边无声响　不见娘子枉费心	Maybe behind the bamboo fence
屋旁还有纸窗在	Let me knock at the door
我隔窗向内看分明	Why there's no response
哎呀，窗口高来看不见	It's so silent inside
有了！垫块石头就看得清	Is what I do all in vain
文秀举目向内望　只见一间小草房	Oh let me try the paper windowpane
小小香台朝上摆　破木交椅分两旁	So that I can view the room with my eyes
三支清香炉中插　荤素菜肴桌上放	Oh, my god! The window is so high
第一碗白鲞红炖天堂肉	Hey, the rock beside could give me a hand
第二碗油煎鱼儿扑鼻香	Let me see, let me see
第三碗香蕈蘑菇炖豆腐	How shabby the room is
第四碗白菜香干炒千张	The little burner's in the middle
第五碗酱烧胡桃浓又浓	The shaky armchairs are on both sides
第六碗酱油花椒醉花生	I can smell the fragrance of the incense
白饭一碗酒一杯	I can see a table of food prepared for a "dead" me
桌上筷子有一双	Fried fish, Heaven meat,
看起来　果然为我做三周年	Mushroom, to-fu, Chinese leaves
感谢你娘子情义长	Walnuts, peanuts, rice, wine, chopsticks
	How touching my Three-year Mourning is!

Assignment 8 Pair Interpretation Tasks

8 – A 中国传统服饰

中国古代服饰最基本的样式是上衣下裳分体着装。道家思想认为天地的颜色为天玄地黄，所以相对应的衣服的颜色也是上玄下黄。到了汉代，上襦下裳、交领右衽、钟袖博带成为当时礼服的典型特征。那时女士穿的曲裾最有特色，是一种穿出来有螺旋状裙边的裙子。由于中国封建社会等级森严，家族观念强烈，人们在服饰上也体现了严内外、辨亲疏、明贵贱、别尊卑的特征。也就是说，社会地位越高的人衣服的用料越多，款式越讲究。家居场合和外出场合的服装、社会地位高和社会地位低的人的服装，主人和仆人的服装均有严格区别。这种风俗对现代社会最大的影响表现在葬礼服饰上，通常直系亲属穿的丧服要比旁系亲属的丧服更复杂。丝绸虽然是中国人最早的发明之一，但在古代也是奢侈的衣料。由于其质地柔软舒适，但是不够经久耐穿，现在多用于制作睡衣。目前男士的中山装和女士的旗袍被认为是经典的中式社交礼服。

8 – B 中国戏曲艺术

中国的戏曲是一种综合性的古典表演形式。和西方的歌剧不同的是，它不仅含有对白、独白、演唱，还含有舞蹈、武术、杂技甚至哑剧。演员的每一个动作都是精心设计的，并且表达的意义都是程式化的。即便是中国人，如果不系统学习，也很难全部理解。中国的戏曲一般以方言区为基础，各自流行。一般认为，昆曲是百戏之祖，最古老、高雅，也最难懂。京剧的流行范围最广，是中国第一大剧种。剧本一般以帝王将相题材的正剧为主，深受老年观众喜爱。第二大剧种是流行于华东地区的越剧，讲述的多是才子佳人的爱情故事。越剧里几乎所有的角色都由漂亮的女演员扮演。现在改良的越剧音乐和配器很有现代感，美术设计既时尚又唯美，比较受年轻学生和女性观众的喜爱。中国戏曲的人物造型包括头、面化妆和服装，化妆和换服装非常麻烦，一般要有专业人员协助才能完成。不信，您一会儿可以体验一下。

 # Appendix

Appendix A Seminar Project

Appendix B Pole-play Test Paper

Appendix C Key to Exercises

Appendix D Course Assessment

Appendix A Seminar Project

Chinese Culture & Life
Chairperson: Course Tutor
Participants: Students of This Class
Presentation time allowed for each project group is 30 minutes.
For each group, there will be 5 minutes to answer the audience' questions if necessary.
Venue: _____
Time: _____

Requirements

1. The group project report should be submitted on the day when you give your presentation in class.

2. Each group member is required to share equal workload in your group work and be responsible for part of the presentation in terms of your own individual work assigned to you in your project.

3. The number of the pages you submitted as your project report should not be less than the number of your group members but your presentation time needs to be controlled under reasonable time limit.

4. Multimedia demos are encouraged in your presentation and relevant illustrations, charts, graphs, figures etc. are also rewarding points to your paper work.

5. Whatever the artistic means have been adopted in your paper work, topic relevance and function relevance are the two fundamental criteria you should keep in mind all the time.

Questions

1. What is the administrative division in China? What's the difference between

municipalities and special administrative regions and autonomous regions? Please recommend ten tourist destinations to your fellow classmates and state their most typical attractions as well as your reasons of recommendation in your group presentation.

2. Discuss and explain the following terms with your group members, "red envelope", "sedan-chair", "Chinese knot". Can you think of other typical Chinese things? To the process of world civilization, what recognized achievements are made by ancient Chinese and why they can be spread throughout the world? Please select ten ancient Chinese achievements and state the reasons of your choice to your fellow classmates.

3. What magic power makes the Chinese culture become sustained civilization? Apart from our current territory, what other countries are greatly influenced by Chinese culture? How do you know? Please gather the information of the Chinese culture satellite countries in Asia and present the facts of the influence of Chinese culture on these countries' tourist attractions.

4. In Beijing, many foreign tourists find many local snacks quite similar to Arabian snacks, what are the snacks? Why? What is the usual serving procedure of a typical Chinese dinner or banquet? What is most special to many western tourists in having Chinese dinner? Please do a group project with your group members and report your findings to your fellow classmates.

5. If you are invited to provide advice on the China-town project in a foreign country, what typical and indispensable elements should be involved in? Please discuss the planning scheme with your group members and present your statement to your fellow classmates.

6. What historical or legendary figures from China are most well-known overseas? Why? Please select ten influential figures and present their stories and your reasons of choice to your fellow classmates.

7. Do Chinese people still wear traditional clothes? Do they have national costume now? How do you think of the traditional Chinese clothes? Someone proposed to have Han-fu, the ceremonial suit of Chinese delegation team in Olympic Games or other occasions, how do you think of this idea, why? Please state your justifications in your presentation.

小组项目分组工作表

班级：

	组员1	组员2	组员3	组员4	组员5	组员6	组员7	组员8
第一组								
第二组								
第三组								
第四组								
第五组								
第六组								
第七组								
第八组								

Appendix B Role-play Test Paper

Test 1-1 Role-play: Hotel Service (I)

每组按要求表演全部场景，时间15分钟，每位考生至少扮演一次饭店员工，一次客人，2—3人一场。

Items	Tasks	Scenarios	Roles
Reservation, Reception & Operator	1-1 团队预订	和平鸽国旅计调来电订房：2017年5月9日—14日，美国团18人下午4点抵店，五间双标间，两间大床房，一间三人间，一间单人间，本社地陪吴浩	计调：张磊 散客甲：Helen/Tony Swan 前台接待甲
	1-2 散客改定	散客甲原定2017年5月6日—11日的入住时间改为5月9日离店，三人间改双标间	
	2-1 信用卡结账	散客乙携眷无预订入住两晚，大床房加童床1549房。房费人民币750元/晚含双早，加床150元/晚，护照登记，信用卡结账，给房卡	散客甲： Helen/Tony Swan 散客乙： Lisa/Eric Brown 前台接待乙
	2-2 无预订入住	散客甲2017年5月6日—9日现金结账，双标间1507房，房费人民币689元/晚含双早，共计2067元	
	2-3 转接国际长途	接听散客乙房间来电，要求接通至东京国际长途叫人电话，对方号码37650432	
	3-1 团队入住	和平鸽国旅美国团18人下午4点抵店，已预订2017年5月9日—14日五间双标间，两间大床房，一间三人间，一间单人间，本社地陪吴浩，公司账户结账，安排次日叫早，时间6:30	导游：吴浩 来电人： Judy/John Smith 前台接待丙
	3-2 电话留言	接听外线电话请求转接1549房散客乙，无人接听，留言请给泰国曼谷Judy/John Smith回话，有要事告之，号码对方已知	

续表

Items	Tasks	Scenarios	Roles
Reservation, Reception & Operator	4-1 结账	和平鸽国旅美国团公司账户结账，导游吴浩签单	导游：吴浩 散客乙： Lisa/Eric Brown 前台接待甲
	4-2 换房	散客乙至前台投诉房间临街太吵，淋浴喷头和马桶不好用。调房至三人间1390房	
Concierge & Housekeeping	5-1 开房	行李员引导散客丙一行两人入住1428房。	散客丙： Jenny/George Cook 行李员 客房服务员
	5-2 开床	客房服务员为其提供开床服务	
	5-3 投诉	散客丙发现空调不好用，投诉，客房服务员承诺找工程人员维修	
	5-4 洗衣服务	散客丙从包中掏出一只脏毛绒玩具熊请求协助快速清洗，客房服务员引导其填写洗衣单并将玩具装袋带走	
	6-1 物品寄存	晚上7点，1428房散客丙至礼宾部寄存摄像机和笔记本电脑，第二天晚上10点取	散客丙： Jenny/George Cook 礼宾接待 行李员
	6-2 信息咨询	散客丙咨询饭店附近是否有地方特色的旅游景观、风味餐厅，到哪里购买相机存储卡。礼宾部为其提供口头咨询和有关旅游指南小册子	
	6-3 代叫的士	散客丙请求代叫出租车，礼宾接待安排行李员协助打车	

Test 1-2 Role-play: Hotel Service (II)

每组按要求表演全部场景，时间15分钟，每位考生至少扮演一次饭店员工、一次客人，2—3人一场。

Items	Tasks	Scenarios	Roles
Restaurant Service	1-1 团队订桌	万福饭店熊猫餐厅接和平鸽国旅计调订餐电话：2017年10月28日，新加坡团18人晚6点晚餐两桌，400元一桌团队餐，三位穆斯林女客，望订无烟区，本社地陪吴浩签单结账	餐厅前台甲 计调：张磊
	1-2 送餐预订	1243房间客人甲致电前台：因要外出看京剧，故订明晚夜宵，10:30—11:00送餐。推荐15元夜宵套餐：绿豆粥、肉夹馍、四川泡菜、杏仁豆腐	餐厅前台乙 客人甲： Helen/Tony Swan
	1-3 散客点菜	和平鸽国旅客人乙一家三口脱团晚归，来餐厅单点晚餐。领班协助点菜：推荐三人用88元经济套餐，菜品包括大丰收、番茄蛋汤、青椒牛肉、宫保鸡丁、米饭、水果沙拉	餐厅领班 客人乙： Lisa/Eric Chiang
Business Center Convention Service	2-1 传真、复印	客人丙携公文夹至中心复印资料。第35—40页、第46—52页共印5份，A4纸。将另一份文件共三页发传真至韩国首尔。复印2元一张，传真费96元，结算刷中国银联信用卡	商务中心甲 客人丙： Anna/Peter Xu
	2-2 票务服务	客人丁至万福饭店商务中心预订2017年10月28去上海的机票三张，中午以后起飞，公务舱，马上出票，信用卡刷票款人民币4 800元。望送至1507房梁女士收。梁女士今晚（6月22日）7点左右入住	商务中心乙 客人丁： Lucy/Richard Pan
	2-3 会场预订	康健家私公司秘书李焕电话预订万福饭店小型会议室，10人开公司高层会。2017年10月28日下午2点至5点。饭店贵宾室报价400元/小时，含免费饮料茶点。约当面细谈	商务中心丙 李焕
Health Recreation Shopping Service	3-1 引导服务	客人戊至康体中心前台希望游泳。服务员告之泳池维修不开放，推荐保龄、桑拿、健身房、卡拉OK、美容美发。客人看到网球场广告希望前往，服务员告之需提前预订。服务员帮忙打电话确认后告之有空位	康体中心 客人戊： Lydia/George Watson
	3-2 购物服务	客人已预购中国特色礼品送给家人、老师、亲戚、朋友（分别爱好音乐、美术、体育）。推荐风筝、年画、丝巾、毽子、民乐CD、玩具熊猫。结账时告之不收外币现金，请客人到大堂兑换人民币。随后客人决定用信用卡结账	商店导购 客人己： Allen/Julia Black

Vocabulary

和平鸽国旅　Dove Travel International

毛绒熊　teddy bear

相机存储卡　SD card

摄像机　camcorder

笔记本电脑　laptop

旅游景观　tourist attraction

地方风味　local-flavor

Test 2-1 Role-play: Guiding Service (I)

Please role play the following scenarios in order. Each group is given 10–15 minutes only. Sharing roles is allowed if no omission of the scenarios.

场　景	角　色	任　务
A Meeting at the Hotel Lobby	Local guide: 张威 Escort: Alan/Linda White	1. 认找旅游团 2. 核对人数——8男、10女、2女童 3. 介绍导游 4. 确认行李 5. 介绍饭店设施
B Check-in Procedure	Escort: Alan/Linda White, Receptionist: 李蒙	1. 问好 2. 收护照 3. 入住登记 4. 信用卡预授权冻结房费 5. 拿钥匙派房
C Shopping Service	Salesperson: 王征 Customer: Lucy/Tony Brown	1. 问好 2. 买地图 3. 买电话卡 4. 买相机存储卡 5. 买雨伞
D Room Service	House Keeper: 刘彬 Guest: Katy/Daniel Black	1. 问好 2. 电话约送水 3. 找被子 4. 调龙头 5. 电话约送餐

Test 2-2 Role-play: Tour Guide Service (II)

Please role play the following scenarios in order. Each group is given 10–15 minutes only. Sharing roles is allowed if no omission of the scenarios.

场 景	角 色	任 务
E FAM Trip Itinerary Negotiation Meeting	Local guide: 张威 National guide: 王佳 Escort: Alan/Linda White Tourist: Katy/Daniel Black	1. 领队介绍到会来宾 2. 全陪线路介绍 3. 地陪线路介绍 4. 领队、游客提问
F Local Family Dinner Experience Tour	Local guide: 张威 National guide: 王佳 Escort: Alan/Linda White Host/hostess: 刘磊 Tourist: Katy/Daniel Black	1. 问好 2. 地陪接洽 3. 主人介绍菜品 4. 领队、游客提问

复习提示：

（1）小组讨论并自行设计为期 15 天的中国游。

（2）合理安排 4—5 个城市及中转交通，简要介绍亮点与设计思路。

（3）选一熟悉城市进行 3—4 天游程设计，含吃、住、行、游、购、娱各要素。

（4）菜单按实际用餐人数设计合理菜品与菜量。

（5）菜谱需含凉、热、主菜、主食、酒水和甜品。

（6）特色菜品需简要介绍。

（7）领队、客人均需互动提问。

（8）合理使用幻灯图片演示。

（9）自备道具加分。

Role Assignment Worksheet for Rople-play

Name	Role 1	Role 2	Role 3
1			
2			
3			
4			
5			
6			
7			
8			

Signature of Director: **Date:**

Role Assignment Worksheet for Role-play

Name	Role 1	Role 2	Role 3
1			
2			
3			
4			
5			
6			
7			
8			

Signature of Director: **Date:**

（此工作表一式两份，一份上交考官备案，另一份各小组自行留底）

Test Assessment Sample Worksheet for Role-play

　　　　　　　　　　　　　　　　　　　　　　　学年度第　　学期

姓名	角色	完整性（5分）	准确性（5分）	流利性（5分）	交互性（5分）	总分（20分）
1						
2						
3						
4						
5						
6						
7						
8						

评语：

考官签字：

日期：

评分标准：

　　完整性（5分）：内容覆盖主要考点；完整切题；无重大遗漏和顺序错误。

　　准确性（5分）：发音正确；用词准确；语法比较符合英文表达习惯。

　　流利性（5分）：语言表达熟练；自动纠错；过渡自然；无严重停顿、口吃。

　　交互性（5分）：语速、音量适中；语言通俗直观；幽默生动；成员间配合默契。

Appendix C Key to Exercises

Unit 1

Key to Listening Extract 1 悉尼机场

（1）Overbooking.

（2）18 kg.

（3）There's paperwork in it that he needs on the plane.

（4）He takes something out.

（5）He has an important meeting in Berlin which he can't miss.

（6）No, all airlines follow the same policy.

（7）Wait until 8:30 to see if he can get on this flight. If not, he will be put on the next flight.

（8）She's responsible for this flight and will call the supervisor to look after people who have to wait for the next one.

（9）Keep it. If they can put him on this flight, they'll take it back. If not, he'll have to check it in again.

Key to Supplementary Reading Extract 1 车上导游欢迎词

（1）C （2）D （3）C

Key to Vocabulary Workshop 词汇识记

1. 新加坡 Singapore	2. 泰国 Thailand	3. 马来西亚 Malaysia	4. 菲律宾 Philippines	5. 印度尼西亚 Indonesia
6. 韩国 Korea	7. 日本 Japan	8. 越南 Viet Nam	9. 柬埔寨 Cambodia	10. 尼泊尔 Nepal
11. 印度 India	12. 斯里兰卡 Sri Lanka	13. 马尔代夫 Maldives	14. 文莱 Brunei	15. 蒙古 Mongolia
16. 中国 China	17. 牙买加 Jamaica	18. 加拿大 Canada	19. 美国 The U. S. A.	20. 古巴 Cuba
21. 墨西哥 Mexico	22. 秘鲁 Peru	23. 巴西 Brazil	24. 南非 South Africa	25. 埃及 Egypt
26. 新西兰 New Zealand	27. 澳大利亚 Australia	28. 挪威 Norway	29. 瑞典 Sweden	30. 冰岛 Iceland
31. 芬兰 Finland	32. 丹麦 Denmark	33. 波兰 Poland	34. 捷克 Czech Republic	35. 匈牙利 Hungary
36. 俄罗斯 Russia	37. 德国 Germany	38. 瑞士 Switzerland	39. 奥地利 Austria	40. 法国 France
41. 卢森堡 Luxembourg	42. 比利时 Belgium	43. 荷兰 Netherlands	44. 英国 Great Britain	45. 爱尔兰 Ireland
46. 土耳其 Turkey	47. 葡萄牙 Portugal	48. 西班牙 Spain	49. 意大利 Italy	50. 希腊 Greece
51. 东京 Tokyo	52. 京都 Kyoto	53. 大阪 Osaka	54. 首尔 Seoul	55. 新德里 New Delhi
56. 曼谷 Bangkok	57. 雅加达 Jakarta	58. 马尼拉 Manila	59. 开罗 Cairo	60. 开普敦 Cape Town
61. 柏林 Berlin	62. 慕尼黑 Munich	63. 法兰克福 Frankfurt	64. 维也纳 Vienna	65. 巴黎 Paris
66. 罗马 Rome	67. 威尼斯 Venice	68. 米兰 Milan	69. 苏黎世 Zurich	70. 伯尔尼 Bern
71. 哥本哈根 Copenhagen	72. 奥斯陆 Oslo	73. 赫尔辛基 Helsinki	74. 雷克雅未克 Reykjavik	75. 斯德哥尔摩 Stockholm
76. 雅典 Athens	77. 圣彼得堡 St. Petersburg	78. 莫斯科 Moscow	79. 都柏林 Dublin	80. 伦敦 London

81. 爱丁堡 Edinburgh	82. 苏格兰 Scotland	83. 曼彻斯特 Manchester	84. 渥太华 Ottawa	85. 多伦多 Toronto
86. 温哥华 Vancouver	87. 华盛顿 Washington	88. 纽约 New York	89. 夏威夷 Hawaii	90. 洛杉矶 Los Angeles
91. 旧金山 San Francisco	92. 波士顿 Boston	93. 芝加哥 Chicago	94. 西雅图 Seattle	95. 拉斯维加斯 Las Vegas
96. 里约热内卢 Rio de Janeiro	97. 悉尼 Sydney	98. 堪培拉 Canberra	99. 墨尔本 Melbourne	100. 惠灵顿 Wellington
101. 基督教 Christianity	102. 天主教 Catholicism	103. 东正教 Orthodox Christianity	104. 大教堂 Cathedral	105. 大主教 Archbishop
106. 新教牧师 Priest of Protestanism	107. 耶稣基督 Jesus Christ	108. 梵蒂冈 Vatican City	109. 圣母 Virgin Mary	110. 三位一体 Trinity
111. 教皇 Pope	112. 耶路撒冷 Jerusalem	113. 管风琴/手风琴 pipe organ/accordian	114. 唱诗班（合唱团）/钢琴 choir/piano	115. 圣经 Bible
116. 穆斯林 Muslim	117. 伊斯兰教 Islamism	118. 麦加 Mecca	119. 清真寺 mosque	120. 古兰经 Quran
121. 庙宇 temple	122. 城堡 castle	123. 祭坛 altar	124. 宫殿 palace	125. 陵寝 mausoleum
126. 纪念堂/纪念碑 memorial hall/monument	127. 温泉/水疗 hot spring/spa	128. 雕塑/喷泉 sculpture/fountain	129. 故居/别墅 old house/villa	130. 水坝/河堤/运河 dam/causeway/canal
131. 大西洋 Atlantic Ocean	132. 北冰洋 Arctic Ocean	133. 太平洋 Pacific Ocean	134. 印度洋 Indian Ocean	135. 亚洲 Asia
136. 欧洲 Europe	137. 非洲 Africa	138. 北美洲 North America	139. 南美洲 South America	140. 大洋洲 Oceania
141. 南极洲 Antarctic	142. 岛/屿 island/islet	143. 半岛/群岛 peninsula/archipelago	144. 海角 cape	145. 海湾 gulf
146. 彩虹 rainbow	147. 瀑布 waterfall	148. 高原/平原 plateau/plain	149. 江河/溪流 river/stream	150. 热带雨林 rain forest

续表

151. 溶洞	152. 潮汐	153. 火山	154. 丹霞地貌	155. 冰山/冰川/雪山
karst cave	tide	volcano	danxia landform	iceberg/glacier/snow-capped mountain
156. 海市蜃楼	157. 沙漠	158. 隧道	159. 山脊/山坡	160. 林荫大道
mirage	desert	tunnel	mountain ridge/mountain slope	boulevard
161. 赤道	162. 海洋公园	163. 游乐场	164. 动物园	165. 植物园
equator	ocean park	recreation park	zoo	botanical garden
166. 台湾海峡/英吉利海峡	167. 海岸/海滩/沙滩	168. 塔/阁/亭/厅/廊/室/台/楼	169. 牛津/剑桥	170. 哈佛/耶鲁
Taiwan Strait/English Channel	coast/beach/sand	pagoda/tower/pavilion/hall/arcade/chamber/terrace/building	Oxford/Cambridge	Harvard/Yale
171. 大学/学院/研究所	172. 研究院/音乐学院	173. 学部/系/研究生院	174. 斯坦福/麻省理工	175. 海德堡/哥廷根/莱比锡
university/college/institute	academy/conservatory	faculty/department/graduate school	Stanford/MIT	Heidelberg/Göttingen/Leipzig
176. 悉尼歌剧院	177. 埃菲尔铁塔	178. 阿尔卑斯山	179. 尼亚加拉瀑布	180. 巴黎圣母院
Sydney Opera House	Eiffel Tower	The Alps	Niagara Falls	Notre Dame de Paris
181. 二条城	182. 大王宫	183. 白金汉宫	184. 斗兽场	185. 维也纳金色大厅
Nijo-jo Castle	Grand Palace	Buckingham Palace	Colosseum	Vienna Golden Hall
186. 美人鱼像	187. 卢浮宫	188. 凯旋门	189. 枫丹白露	190. 埃及金字塔
Mermaid	Louvre	Arch of Triumph	Château de Fontainebleau	Egyptian Pyramids

Key to Interpretation Tasks 导游欢迎词英译汉

大家好。希望大家都能听我讲一下。

我叫玛丽，明天上午的市容观光我们一共有三位本地导游陪同您步行游览，另两位导游分别是彼得和翠茜。

游览于十点整开始，大概要用两个小时。我们将在饭店门口外集合，然后分成三个小团，这样您更容易听清讲解。

如果您没有防水的连帽风衣，我建议您带上雨衣或雨伞，因为预报天气情况不太好。如果有可能，您要穿厚实点的步行鞋。

别忘记带相机，因为有很多拍照的机会。我们先参观教堂，然后徒步穿过植物园，最后去水果蔬菜市场转一转。这段路我们会经过战争纪念遗址并沿河而行。

游览活动最后在位于主广场的莎士比亚茶室结束，您可以在那里品尝一块大名鼎鼎的丹地果仁糕。

翠茜导游是位历史专家。因此，如果哪位对历史细节感兴趣我建议您加入她的团，您定会大饱耳福的。

还要再提醒您一句。教堂上午有宗教活动，所以我们到那里后您一定得保持安静不要打扰那些祷告的教徒。

如果哪位想要我们在这个城市的参访行程，过后我很乐意给您提供一份。

如果您还想了解我们城市更多的迷人之处，对这里精美的建筑与古迹感兴趣，有插图版导游书在前台出售，售价2.5英镑。

衷心祝各位旅游愉快，明天上午十点整见，千万别迟到!

Unit 2

Key to Listening Extract 2 海角格蕾丝酒店（上）

(1) d (2) c (3) f (4) a (5) g (6) h (7) e (8) b

Key to Listening Extract 3 詹姆斯国王酒店（上）

3.1 (1) f (2) c (3) g (4) e (5) a

3.2 (1) 15th July   (2) 2
   (3) Herridge   (4) Ann
   (5) 2   (6) none
   (7) 25 Oldham Road, Manchester
   (8) DBL   (9) non-smoking
   (10) 205   (11) £110 per person
   (12) bottle of champagne in room on arrival
   (13) yes   (14) 103
   (15) VISA   (16) 4999 1825 6857 6238

Key to Listening Extract 4 詹姆斯国王酒店（下）

(1) 6/12   (2) 8/12   (3) 19
(4) £95 per night incl. Breakfast   (5) double room with a bath
(6) Urbanik   (7) Polish
(8) EG6662781

Key to Listening Extract 5 圣彼得堡元帅酒店

(1) A chicken sandwich and a pot of coffee
(2) In the hotel information pack in each room
(3) His wife in UK
(4) Because they are made via satellite
(5) 10,783 rubles
(6) By cash

Key to Listening Extract 6 霍顿夫人投诉（上）

(1) g (2) c (3) e (4) a (5) b (6) f (7) d

Key to Listening Extract 7 霍顿夫人投诉（下）

(1) It was either lost or stolen.

（2）Where his wife is.

（3）The necklace was mislaid while moving rooms and the housekeeper searched the first room but was unable to find the necklace.

（4）His wife has been moved to a different room.

（5）The switchboard didn't know that the room had been changed.

Key to Vocabulary Workshop 词汇识记

1. 预订	2. 登记/登记簿	3. 入住手续	4. 退房手续	5. 前台
booking/reservation	registration/register	check-in	check-out	front desk reception
6. 收银	7. 行李车	8. 礼宾部	9. 问询处	10. 货币兑换
cashier	luggage cart	concierge	information/enquiry	currency exchange
11. 失物招领	12. 贵重物品	13. 寄存/押金	14. 投诉	15. 房费
lost property helpdesk	valuables	deposit	complain	room charge
16. 退款/扣除	17. 衣帽间	18. 房价表	19. 打折	20. 宣传册
refund/deduction	cloakroom	room rate tariff	discount	pamphlet / brochure / booklet
21. 信用卡	22. 现金	23. 旅行支票	24. 报销	25. 饭店名片
credit card	cash	traveler's cheque	reimburse	hotel business card
26. 酒吧	27. 自助餐	28. 现点	29. 套餐	30. 宴会
bar	buffet	à la carte	table d'hort	banquet
31. 食堂	32. 餐厅/餐馆	33. 便利店	34. 送餐服务	35. 精品廊
cafeteria	dinning hall/restaurant	convenience store	room service	shopping arcade
36. 双人标间	37. 单人间	38. 婴儿床	39. 套间	40. 大床房
twin room	single room	baby-cot	suite	double room
41. 贵宾室/会议室	42. 记者会	43. 分机/长途/国际长途	44. 传真/电话亭	45. 太平门/紧急出口
VIP reception room/ conference room	press conference	extension/long-distance call/international call	fax (faximile)/ telephone booth	emergency exit

续表

46. 商务中心	47. 上网接口	48. 打印/复印	49. 门禁电话	50. 信封/包裹
business center	Internet access	print/copy	intercom	envelope/parcel
51. 前台服务员	52. 客房服务员	53. 餐厅服务员	54. 值班经理	55. 门童/行李员
receptionist	housemaid / housekeeper	waiter/waitress	duty manager	bell boy / doorman / busboy / porter
56. 房卡/餐券	57. 收据/发票	58. 手纸	59. 男/女厕所	60. 厕所/马桶
room card/coupon	receipt/invoice	toilet paper	man's room/lady's room	bathroom/toilet
61. 台盆/龙头	62. 干手器	63. 镜子/梳子	64. 拖鞋/鞋擦	65. 熨斗/衣架
sink/faucet/tap	hand dryer	mirror/comb	slippers/shoe polisher	iron/hanger
66. 转换插头	67. 吹风机	68. 剃须刀/膏	69. 万用插座	70. 遥控器
traveller's adapter	hairdrier	shaving razor/ shaving cream	all-purpose outlet	remote controller
71. 洗手液	72. 洗衣袋	73. 花洒/浴缸	74. 香皂/香水	75. 纸巾/湿巾
handwash fluid	laundry bag	shower/bathtub	soap / perfume	napkin/wet tissue
76. 洗面奶	77. 洗发水	78. 护发素	79. 沐浴液	80. 润肤露
facial foam	shampoo	hair conditioner	bath gel	body lotion
81. 浴巾/浴帽	82. 唇膏	83. 棉签	84. 针线包	85. 牙刷/牙膏
bath towel/shower cap	lip balm	cotton swab	sewing kits	tooth brush/tooth paste
86. 被子	87. 床罩	88. 床单	89. 毯子	90. 床垫
quilt/duvet	bedspread	bed sheet	blanket	mattress
91. 地毯	92. 靠垫	93. 枕头	94. 空调	95. 冰箱/冰柜
carpet/rug	cushion	pillow	aircon/air conditioner	refrigerator (fridge)/freezer
96. 饮水机	97. 电水壶	98. 电视	99. 台式电脑	100. 手提电脑
water dispenser	electric pot	TV set	desktop computer	laptop
101. 开关	102. 台灯	103. 断电/充电	104. 维修	105. 客房酒柜
switch	desk lamp	power off/recharge	maintenance	mini-bar

续表

106. 租借	107. 婴儿车	108. 轮椅	109. 雨伞/拐杖	110. 大堂
rent/lease	pram	wheelchair	umbrella/cane	lobby
111. 送餐车	112. 投影仪	113. 大屏幕	114. 扩音器	115. 麦克风
breakfast cart	projector	projection screen	amplifier	microphone
116. 叫早服务	117. 票务中心	118. 按摩	119. 医务室	120. 康乐中心
morning call	ticket center	massage	clinic	recreation center
121. 急救	122. 男女发廊	123. 电梯	124. 扶梯/直梯	125. 柜台
first-aid	beauty salon/barber's shop	elevator	escalator/lift	counter

Unit 3

Key to Listening Extract 8 法式风味餐厅

8.1

（1）Kir

（2）The man possibly went there for a working lunch a few years before.

（3）French onion soup and snails.

（4）Because it is typically French.

（5）Rack of lamb.

（6）She asks for the lamb without the mint sauce.

（7）Béarnaise sauce with tomato purée.

（8）A bottle Cabernet Sauvignon.

8.2

（1）If you would like to

（2）Take your coat

（3）Here's the

（4）Something to drink before your meal

（5）Are you ready to

（6）And what would you like

（7）I'd certainly recommend

（8）So that's

Key to Vocabulary Workshop 词汇识记

1. 四川泡菜	2. 小葱拌豆腐	3. 北京豆酱	4. 大丰收	5. 冷荤拼盘
Sichuan pickles	tofu salad with chives	Peking soybean jelly	great harvest salad	sausage assortment
6. 宫保鸡丁	7. 黑椒牛柳	8. 糖醋里脊	9. 鱼香肉丝	10. 烤乳猪
kung-pao chicken	beef fillet with black peppercorn	pork fillet with sweet and sour sauce	stir-fried pork shreds with Sichuan chilli sauce	roast piglet
11. 清蒸鲥鱼	12. 红烧狮子头	13. 蚝油生菜	14. 番茄炒鸡蛋	15. 香菇油菜
steamed shad	soy-sauce braised meatball	stir-fried lettuce with oyster sauce	scrambled eggs with sliced tomato	stir-fried pak choy with black mushroom
16. 炸酱面	17. 扬州炒饭	18. 鸡丝凉面	19. 肠粉/春卷	20. 星洲米粉
fried soysauce noodle	Yangzhou stir-fried rice	cold noodle with sesame sauce & chicken shreds	rice paper roll / spring roll	stir-fried rice vermicelli in Singapore style
21. 莲藕排骨汤	22. 北京烤鸭	23. 杏仁豆腐	24. 蟹黄豆腐羹	25. 拔丝山药
pork chop soup with lotus root	Peking roast duck	cold almond jelly	crab roe tofu soup	long yam in hot toffee
26. 红豆粥	27. 皮蛋肉粥	28. 绿豆粥	29. 小米粥	30. 汤圆
azuki porridge	porridge with preserved egg cubes	mung bean porridge	millet porridge	boiled glutinous ball
31. 烧卖	32. 小笼包	33. 肉夹馍	34. 褡裢火烧	35. 驴肉烧饼
shao-mai	steamed dumpling	Chinese hamburger	Peking fried roll	donkey meat hamburger
36. 年糕	37. 粽子	38. 煎饼	39. 羊肉串	40. 豆浆
new year's cake	glutinous rice pyramid	Chinese paper-thin pancake	mutton kebab	soy milk
41. 饺子	42. 金银馒头	43. 馄饨	44. 土豆泥	45. 茶汤
boiled dumpling	steamed and fried bun assortment	wanton	potato paste	flour soup

续表

46. 烤香肠	47. 爆米花	48. 蛋挞	49. 糖葫芦	50. 麻辣烫
grilled sausage	popcorn	custard tart	sugar-coated fruit crispy	chilli kebab hotch potch
51. 冰棍儿	52. 汽水	53. 凉茶	54. 芝麻糊	55. 鸡蛋羹
popsicle/ice pop	soda water	Chinese herbal tea	sweet black sesame soup	chawanmushi

Unit 4

Key to Listening Extract 9 销售免税品

（1）50 milliliters　　　　　　（2）$43.30
（3）Leopard, teddy bear　　（4）Teddy bear
（5）$57.90

Key to Listening Extract 10 海角格蕾丝酒店（下）

（1）Go shopping in the city's center.
（2）Large amounts of cash.
（3）In the safe deposit box in their room.
（4）Keep doors locked at all times.
（5）The poorer areas of the city.
（6）Robben Island.

Key to Vocabulary Workshop 词汇识记

1. 珐琅	2. 景泰蓝	3. 水晶	4. 玉石	5. 玛瑙
enamel	cloisonné enamel	crystal	jade	agate
6. 琥珀	7. 象牙	8. 珍珠	9. 钻石	10. 珊瑚
amber	ivory	pearl	diamond	coral

续表

11. 耳钉/耳环	12. 手镯	13. 胸针/胸花	14. 吊坠/项链	15. 发夹/发卡
ear studs/ear rings	bracelet	brooch/bouquet	pendent/locket（盒状吊坠）crucifix（十字架）necklace	hairpin / ornamental pin / hair ribbon / headband / hair clasp
16. 领带夹	17. 袖扣	18. 首饰盒	19. 铜	20. 青铜/黄铜
tie clip	cuff-links	jewelry box	copper	bronze/brass
21. 铂金	22. 银	23. 黄金	24. 毛笔	25. 墨
platinum	silver	gold	Chinese writing brush (painting brush)	ink stick
26. 宣纸	27. 砚台	28. 文房四宝	29. 书法	30. 国画
writing rice paper	ink slab	Chinese traditional stationery	Chinese calligraphy	Chinese painting
31. 印章	32. 笔筒	33. 镇纸	34. 笔架	35. 内画壶
seal/chop	pen holder	paper weight	Chinese painting brush stand	inner-painted snuff bottle
36. 陶	37. 瓷	38. 紫砂	39. 陶艺	40. 根雕
pottery	porcelain	purple earthen ware	ceramics	root carving
41. 盆景	42. 泥人	43. 面塑	44. 绢人	45. 双面绣
bonsai	clay figurine	dough figurine	silk doll	double-side embroidery
46. 汉字	47. 漆雕	48. 年画	49. 蜡染	50. 剪纸
Chinese character	lacquer carving	new year's painting	batik	paper-cut
51. 风车/风铃	52. 拨浪鼓	53. 不倒翁	54. 中国结	55. 麻将
pinwheel（荷式风车）windwheel（中式风车）windchime/windbell	rattle drum	roly-poly	Chinese knot	mah-jong
56. 风筝	57. 毽子	58. 空竹	59. 鲁班锁	60. 九连环
Kite	Chinese Shuttlecock	Chinese yo-yo	Luban Smart Lock	Chinese Rings

Unit 5

Key to Listening Extract 11 太平洋旅行社

Number of pax: 13 (pax: passengers)

Accommodation: 5 double rooms and 1 triple

Departure date: 24 March

Key to Listening Extract 12 乌克兰之旅

Trip: 10 day trip to Moscow via Odessa Departing from Gatwick 13th July

Insurance: £22 per person

Visa: £17 per person

Deposit: £100 per person

Sum of money on cheque: £278

Key to Listening Extract 13 佛罗里达之旅

(1) self-catering apartment (2) 14
(3) Thursday 17 May (4) Thursday 31 May
(5) 2 (6) Jane Wright, Simon Wright
(7) 1 (8) Andrew Wright

Key to Listening Extract 14 都柏林旅游

(1) Dublinia: multimedia exhibition of mediaeval Dublin

(2) Newgrange: 5000-year-old prehistoric site, burial chamber and the oldest solar observatory

(3) Dublin Writer's Museum: manuscripts, letters and rare editions of Jonathan Swift, Oscar Wilde, James Joyce

(4) O'donoghue's: where the Dubliner's group started up

Key to Listening Extract 15 克拉科旅游

(1) She's attending a conference and is flying back to the UK on Sunday night.

(2) About three hours/a whole morning.

(3) There are long queues.

(4) A cellar bar with cabaret and disco.

（5）She does not want to go dancing.
（6）To go to the pub U Louisa.

Key to Vocabulary Workshop 词汇识记

1. 松树 pine tree	2. 竹 bamboo	3. 腊梅 wintersweet	4. 兰花 orchid	5. 柳树 willow tree
6. 杨树 poplar tree	7. 侧柏 cypress	8. 龙柏 Chinese juniper	9. 洋槐/刺槐 black locust	10. 国槐/龙爪槐 Chinese scholar tree/Japanese pagoda tree
11. 樟木 camphor wood	12. 檀香木 sandal wood	13. 紫檀/花梨 red sandal wood	14. 红木 rosewood	15. 楠木 phoebe wood
16. 桃花 peach flower	17. 合欢 silk tree	18. 荷花/芙蓉 lotus	19. 睡莲 water lily	20. 菊花 chrysanthemum
21. 桂花 sweet olive	22. 美人蕉 canna/Indian shot	23. 石榴 pomegranate	24. 寿桃 longevity peach	25. 蟠桃 flat peach
26. 牡丹 peony	27. 枣 Chinese date	28. 栗子 chestnut	29. 花生 peanut	30. 核桃 walnut
31. 珙桐 dove tree	32. 人参 ginseng	33. 灵芝 longevity fungus	34. 油菜花 rapeseed flower	35. 金丝猴 snub-nosed monkey
36. 小熊猫 red panda	37. 娃娃鱼 giant salamanda	38. 龟 turtle	39. 玳瑁 hawksbill	40. 大熊猫 giant panda
41. 麒麟 kylin (kilin)	42. 虎 tiger	43. 豹 leopard	44. 象 elephant	45. 獬豸 Chinese unicorn
46. 龙 dragon	47. 狮子 lion	48. 水牛 buffalo	49. 黄牛 bull	50. 梅花鹿 sika
51. 蟾蜍 toad	52. 八哥 mynah bird/myna	53. 鹦鹉 parrot	54. 黄鹂 Chinese oriole	55. 鸳鸯 Mandarin ducks
56. 孔雀 peacock	57. 鸿雁 swan goose	58. 仙鹤 longevity crane	59. 燕子 swallow	60. 飞燕/百灵 lark
61. 凤凰 phoenix	62. 喜鹊 magpie	63. 蝙蝠 bat	64. 金鱼 gold fish	65. 鲤鱼 carp

Unit 6

Key to Supplementary Reading Extract 2 古巴游程

第 1 天

周二中午乘坐委航的航班离开伦敦，中停（委内瑞拉首都）加拉加斯，晚间抵达（古巴首都）哈瓦那。直赴位于哈瓦那老城区中央公园对面的广场饭店，该地区素以传统的西班牙风情而闻名。

译者注：VIASA 为委内瑞拉国际航空公司 Venezuelan International Airways 的英文首字母缩写。

第 2—3 天

探访哈瓦那。参观哈瓦那郊区的手工艺品中心，游览瓜纳瓦科阿博物馆，该馆设有受古巴影响的非洲文化专题展室。在哈瓦那老城街道自由漫步并欣赏城市精美建筑，参观革命博物馆、军事要塞旧址及大教堂。

第 4 天

参观雪茄工厂。搭乘航班飞往位于古巴东部的圣地亚哥岛，该岛以建筑和美丽的环境而著称。晚上下榻美洲酒店。

第 5 天

城市观光，包括卡斯特罗和他的追随者们于 1953 年发动军事政变失败的蒙卡达兵营。圣地亚哥较好的博物馆还包括建于 16 世纪的委拉斯开兹的居所和百加得博物馆（自选项目）。

译者注——Casa 在西语中为"房子"的意思，Museo 在西语中为"博物馆"的意思。Velazquez 为 16 世纪时期古巴的统治者。

第 6 天

游览位于圣地亚哥北部 18 英里远乡村的科布里方型教堂，乘飞机返回哈瓦那。下榻广场酒店。

第 7 天

返程回家。

Key to Supplementary Reading Extract 3 冰岛游程

星期四　晚上从伦敦希思罗机场飞抵凯夫拉维克镇。前往（冰岛首都）雷克雅未克市的海岛饭店。

星期五　上午市容观光，下午深度探访或者休闲购物。

星期六　（新年前夜）：上午浏览蓝湖并在奶蓝色的湖水中泡澡。晚上品尝维京海盗宴。午夜有新年焰火表演。在冰岛烧酒（冰岛杜松子酒）的推杯换盏中迎接新年的到来。

星期天　（新年）金圈之旅——一日游线路。离开雷克雅未克经过赫里舍迪关到达温泉城。那里的温室村水果、蔬菜、鲜花都在由地热供暖的温室里生长。游览盖锡尔泉，英文中"间歇泉"就是采用的"盖锡尔"这个词，它的来历就是冰岛的盖锡尔泉。乘车前往世人公认的冰岛最美的瀑布——黄金瀑布。该瀑布分为上下两叠，水流直接倾注到15公里长的深壑峡谷中，这座瀑布每年这个时候都处于冰冻状态。

在珞珈湖畔驻足，蒸腾的水汽从湖边泛起，形成天然的桑拿湖。可以选择在湖中游泳。最后在返回雷克雅未克的路上听导游讲解充满冰岛色彩的传奇故事，晚上安排晚餐。

星期一　返回伦敦。

Key to Listening Extract 16 尼罗河之旅

（1）morning: Giza pyramids

（2）afternoon: Egyptian Museum and the Tutankhamun collection

（3）coach to Temple of Ramses II and the Temple of Hathor

（4）afternoon: flight over Aswan Dam to see dam and unfinished obelisk

（5）overnight on board, ship at Aswan

（6）morning: Visit to West Bank to see Valley of the Kings and Queens and the temple of Hatshepsut

（7）afternoon: Relax before flight back

（8）optional extra few days in Luxor with excursion to Karnak temples

Key to Listening Extract 17 中国之旅

1 Beijing

1.1 The Forbidden City

1.2 The Summer Palace

1.3 The Temple of Heaven

2 Chengde

2.1 The Summer Resort

2.2 Little Potala Palace

2.3 Jin-shan-ling Great Wall

3 Xi'an

4 Xi'an

4.1 Terracotta Warriors

4.2 Huaqing Hot Springs

4.3 Banpo Neolithic Village

5 Suzhou

5.1 Gardens

5.2 Silk Factory

6 Guilin/Yangshuo

6.1 The Lijiang River

6.2 Limestone formations along the river bank

6.3 Cormorant fishermen at work

7 Hong Kong

Key to Listening Extract 18 滑雪冬令营

18.1

（1）Welcome meeting

（2）Cross-country skiing

（3）Snowshoeing

（4）Demonstration of ski equipment

（5）Torchlit descent of the mountain

（6）Party/Karaoke

18.2

（1）In the hotel lounge

（2）Must be over 12 and accompanied by an adult

（3）Snow trekking, wearing 'tennis rackets' on your feet

（4）In the hotel lobby

（5）Advanced skiers

（6）Live band, dancing and karaoke

（7）On the notice-board in the hotel lobby

Key to Vocabulary Workshop 词汇识记

1. 盘古开天	2. 伏羲八卦	3. 女娲补天	4. 精卫填海	5. 共工怒触不周山
God of World Creation	Turtle-snake God / God of Water	Sky-gap-filling Goddess	Fairy Bird Goddess	Mountain Headbutter
6. 祝融火神	7. 神农尝百草	8. 夸父逐日	9. 后羿射日	10. 嫦娥奔月
God of Fire	God of Chinese Herbs	Sun Catcher	Sun Archer	Moon Goddess
11. 仓颉造字	12. 大禹治水	13. 愚公移山	14. 炎黄子孙	15. 玉皇大帝
Creator of Chinese Characters	King of Flood Control	Ambitious Fool Man	Chinese Offsprings	Jade Emperor
16. 瑶池王母	17. 牛郎织女	18. 八仙过海	19. 麻姑献寿	20. 刘海戏金蟾
Jade Empress	Love Story of Cowboy and Girl Weaver	Magic Power of the Eight Immortals	Goddess of Birthday Celebration	Game between Liuhai and Froggy Bank
21. 和合二仙	22. 钟馗嫁妹	23. 五子登科	24. 哪吒闹海	25. 福禄寿三星
Immortals of Harmony & Union	Match-making by the Ghost Judge Brother	Five Promising Boys	Fight between Ne-zha and Dragon Prince	Immortals of Blessing, Fortune and Longevity
26. 高山流水	27. 西施浣纱	28. 昭君出塞	29. 貂蝉拜月	30. 贵妃醉酒
Chinese Soul Mates' Friendship	Beauty of Riverside Laundry	Beauty of Peace-making Marriage	Beauty of Moon Worship	Drunken Beauty
31. 门神	32. 妈祖	33. 龙王	34. 哼哈二将	35. 四大天王
Door Guardians	Sea Goddess	Dragon King	Hum & Haw King Kongs	the Four Lokapalas

36. 弥勒/韦陀	37. 观音菩萨	38. 释迦/如来	39. 文殊/普贤	40. 地藏王
Maitreya (Laughing Buddha)/Veda	Mother Buddha / Goddess of Mercy	Shakyamuni	Shakyamuni's (Right & Left) Bodhisattvas	Ksitigarbha (Great Vow Buddha)
41. 罗汉	42. 飞天	43. 济公	44. 孙悟空	45. 猪八戒
Arhat	Flying Apsaras	Mad Monk	Monkey King	Pigsy
46. 沙和尚	47. 唐僧师徒	48. 孔子	49. 鲁班	50. 华佗
Sandy	Monk Tang & His Three Disciples	Confucius	Master of Carpentry	Magic Doctor
51. 关羽	52. 包拯	53. 诸葛亮	54. 岳飞	55. 郑和
Saint of Righteousness	Saint of Justice	Saint of Wisdom	Saint of Loyalty	Captain Zheng He
56. 八卦	57. 儒家思想	58. 道家思想	59. 佛教	60. 暗八仙
Chinese Hexagrams	Confucianism	Taoism	Buddhism	Weapons of the Eight Immortals

Unit 7

Key to Listening Extract 19　巴塞罗那观光

（1）√　（2）√　（3）√　（4）×　（5）×　（6）√

Key to Listening Extract 20　伦敦自然博物馆

（1）19th-century　　　（2）steel
（3）animals　　　（4）dinosaurs
（5）displays　　　（6）Earth galleries
（7）free　　　（8）cafeteria

Key to Listening Extract 21　瓦韦尔古堡游

（1）c　（2）e　（3）d　（4）b　（5）a

Key to Vocabulary Workshop 词汇识记

1. 腊八 Laba Festival (the 8th Day of the 12th Lunar Month)	2. 除夕 the Chinese New Year's Eve	3. 春节 the Chinese Spring Festival	4. 元宵节 the Lantern Festival	5. 清明节 the Qing Ming Festival
6. 端午节 the Dragon-boat Festival	7. 中秋节 the Mid-autumn Festival	8. 七夕 Chinese St. Valentine's Day	9. 重阳节 the Double-ninth Festival	10. 除尘 house cleaning
11. 祭灶 Kitchen God worship	12. 门神 picture of Door Gods	13. 春联 Spring Festival couplets	14. 灯笼 lantern	15. 包饺子 making Chinese dumplings
16. 爆竹 firecracker	17. 焰火 fireworks	18. 红包 red envelope	19. 舞狮 lion dance	20. 舞龙 dragon dance
21. 扭秧歌 yangko dance	22. 跑旱船 land boat dance	23. 踩高跷 stilts walking	24. 花车巡游 float procession	25. 舞中幡 flagpole stunts
26. 杂技 acrobatic show	27. 魔术 conjuring tricks	28. 腰鼓 waist drum	29. 武术 kung-fu/Chinese martial arts	30. 盛装游行 costume parade
31. 木偶戏 puppet show	32. 皮影戏 shadow play	33. 灯会 lantern fair	34. 花会 flower fair	35. 庙会 temple fair
36. 烧香 incense burning	37. 祭祖 ancestor worship	38. 踏青 spring excursion	39. 荡秋千 having a swing	40. 放风筝 kite-flying
41. 寒食 taking cold meals	42. 放河灯 lantern floating	43. 会船 boat-rowing race	44. 赛龙舟 dragon-boat race	45. 包粽子 making glutinous rice pyramid
46. 吃月饼 eating mooncake	47. 赏月 moon worship	48. 登高 hill-climbing	49. 赏菊 chrysanthemum appreciation	50. 家宴 family dinner
51. 复活节 Easter	52. 母亲节 Mother's Day	53. 感恩节 Thanksgiving Day	54. 圣诞节 Christmas	55. 情人节 St. Valentine's Day
56. 劳动节 Labor Day	57. 青年节 Youth Day	58. 儿童节 Children's Day	59. 妇女节 Women's Day	60. 国庆节 National Day

Key to Pair Interpretation Tasks 双人口译练习

A. Chinese Food Culture

Chinese cuisine generally falls into four categories: Sichuan cuisine, Shandong cuisine, Canton cuisine and Huaiyang cuisine. The traditional eight-course Chinese dinner consists of tea or drink, appetizer, cold dish, side dish, main dish, soup, rice or dim sum, and fruit. Gourmets usually use three criteria to judge the quality of the dish, namely what it looks like, how it smells, and how it tastes. Chinese cuisine is actually very rich in flavors, such as sour, sweet, bitter, spicy and salty. As to each flavor, it has a wide selection of representative dishes. The cooking technique of Chinese cuisine is also complicated, including ingredients selection and match, slicing and cutting skills, seasoning and dressing, flavor mixture and penetration, time and heat control etc. Chinese hotpot is a special way of cooking in Chinese cuisine family. Traditionally, Chinese hotpot goes into two subcategories: the Mongolian hotpot and the Sichuan hotpot. Apart from the plates which western guests use a lot, bowls and chopsticks are also indespensible tableware in Chinese dinners.

B. Chinese Zodiac

Like the 12 zodiac signs in Western culture, there are also 12 zodiac animals in Chinese culture. The 12 western zodiac signs only represent 1 year, while the 12 Chinese zodiac animals represent 12 years. The zodiac calendar has been used in China for thousands of years. The 12 Chinese zodiac animals are mouse, bull, tiger, rabbit, dragon, snake, horse, goat, monkey, rooster, dog and pig. Take myself for example. I was born in the year 1976, and my zodiac sign animal is dragon. You can calculate which sign of the zodiac you were born under, and you may also find many things related to the Chinese zodiac in the souvenir shop. Similar to the astrology in western culture, there was also fortune-tellers in ancient China who were supposed to be able to predict fate for ignorant people. In our country, such belief that people born under certain zodiac animals will not be perfect match in marriage still prevails. However, in modern society, fewer and fewer people believe that superstitious ideas with the spread of scientific rationalism.

C. Chinese Calligraphy and Chinese Painting

Chinese calligraphy and Chinese painting are regarded as the best representative art form embodying the spirit of Chinese cultured people. Although modern science and technology didn't approach the life of ancient Chinese people, this old oriental land was by no means a barbarian place, but a poetic and civilized world. Over 2000 years ago, when China was unfortunately split into several kingdoms, its calligraphy, painting, and poetic essay came up to the first peak. From then on, no matter whether China was a unified country or it went into wartime chaos, people's art enthusiasm seems never to be diminished. As early as 1000 years ago, the Chinese society nearly became the poem world. In the contemporary age of Shakespeare, that was about 500 years ago, Chinese drama reached its first climax. Chinese cultured people tended to devote their personal emotions, whatever joy or sorrow, into their painting strokes. An interesting thing is that many famous ancient Chinese artists were not professionals and some famous poets, artists, calligraphers were even kings or emperors. In ancient Chinese education system, learning poem-writing and painting was widely regarded as an indispensible part of children's personal cultivation. Obviously, China has formed its unique oriental aesthetic system from the very early age.

Unit 8

Key to Listening Extract 22 日本歌舞伎

Noh
Origins 14th
Audience higher social classes
Themes gods, warriors, beautiful women and supernatural beings
Costume masks

Stage   outdoor wooden stage
Music   traditional drums and flutes

Kabuki
Origins   17th century
Audience   ordinary people
Themes   historical events and relationships between men and women
Costume   elaborate, exaggerated make-up
Stage   well-equipped wooden stage with trapdoors and footbridge
Music   n/a

Banraku
Origins   early 17th century
Audience   n/a
Themes   historical events and relationships between men and women
Costume   puppets, the puppeteer wears traditional formal dress
Stage   n/a
Music   traditional music performed on a shamisen

Key to Listening Extract 23 莫斯科观光

Climate:
Warmest in July and August
Summerdays are long, can rain a lot
Snow from November to April

Getting Around:
Easy and cheap
From airport to city center by bus and metro or train
Best to see central area on foot
Other parts, metro is fastest, cheapest and easiest
Buses, trolleybuses and trams where no metro

Sightseeing：

The Kremlin, Red Square and St Basil's Cathedral, Lenin's tomb, Gorky Park

Entertainment:

Moscow Film Festival

Russian Winter Festival

Food & Drink：

Quick snacks — sweet and savory pies, jacket potatoes with fillings, bliny

Key to Vocabulary Workshop 词汇识记

1. 冠	2. 帽	3. 盔	4. 巾	5. 袍
crown	hat	helmet	coverchief	robe
6. 平天冠	7. 凤冠	8. 紫金冠	9. 皇帽	10. 罗帽
emperor's ceremonial crown	phoenix crown	prince's crown	king's hat	servant's hat
11. 乌纱	12. 夫子盔	13. 蝴蝶盔	14. 钻天盔	15. 帅盔
official's hat	general's helmet	lady's helmet	worrior's helmet	commander's helmet
16. 文生巾	17. 道巾	18. 浩然巾	19. 员外巾	20. 观音兜
scholar's casual hat	Toaist priest's hat	Arabian kerchief	lord's casual hat	Mother Buddha's headdress
21. 月牙箍	22. 翎子	23. 虎头靴	24. 高方靴	25. 靠
Buddhist headhoop	pheasant tails	tiger-head boots	high boots	armor
26. 护心镜	27. 靠旗	28. 蟒袍	29. 玉带	30. 官衣
heart-shield mirror	armor flags	dragon robe	jade band	official robe
31. 补子	32. 宫衣	33. 氅	34. 褶子	35. 帔
embroidered patch	palace maid's dress	officer's overcoat	casual overgown	embroidered overdress
36. 箭衣	37. 饭兜	38. 云肩	39. 坎肩	40. 道袍
worrior's suit	apron	lady's short embroidered cape	waistcoat	Toaist robe
41. 法衣	42. 袈裟	43. 斗篷	44. 花脸	45. 髯口
Buddhist undergown	Buddhist cassock	cloak	painted face	artificial whiskers

续表

46. 头面	47. 旗袍	48. 旗头	49. 和服	50. 中山装
costume jewelry & headpiece	cheongsam	Manchurian lady's headdress	kimono	Chinese tunic suit
51. 唐装	52. 上衣下裳	53. 交领右衽	54. 钟袖博带	55. 曲裾
Chinese-style garment	upper coat & lower skirt	y chaped collar & right-side knotting	bell sleeves & wide waistband	spiral dress

Key to Jigsaw Game 汉服曲裾着装程序

Step 3	Step 6	Step 2
Step 5	Step 1	Step 4

Key to Jigsaw Game 中国戏曲旦角化妆程序

Step 4	Step 2	Step 6
Step 3	Step 5	Step 1

Key to Translation Workshop 戏曲剧名翻译

English Names	Representative Arias, Duets, or stunts shows
1. Peking Opera	Would you Mind Listening to Me?My Dear Princess! in The Story of Si-lang Returning Home Night Fight at San Cha Kou The Drunken Beauty
2. Kun Opera	Joking at Family School in The Peony Pavilion
3. Shaoxing Opera	The Schoolmates' Farewell in The Story of Butterfly Lovers
4. Huangmei Opera	Let's Go Home, My Darling! in The Love Story of the Cowboy and the Girl Weaver
5. Yu Opera	Who Says Woman Is Inferior to Man?—Hua Mu-lan
6. Ping Opera	The Song of the Season Flowers—The Flower Match-maker
7. Sichuan Opera	The Mask Change Stunts
8. Shao Opera	The Monkey Stunts

Key to Supplementary Translation Exercise 补充翻译练习

To My Dearest Soul Mate in Saving Dragon Princess

Shu-la-la like the breeze kissing the pinewoods

Xiang-chan-chan as the stream touching the valley

Surely it's just my humble impromptu piece

How did it trickle through her gentle fingers

Oh, my suspended thoughts, my never-ending music

Dear me, how could she make it a masterpiece

I'd thought my soul love was only smiling in my dream

Is that true she comes all the way to my eyes

Key to Pair Interpretation Tasks 双人口译练习

A. Traditional Chinese Garments

Traditional Chinese garment is composed of two parts: upper coat, and lower skirt. The Taoist philosophy believes that the color of the sky is black and the color of the ground is yellow so the color of the human garment should also go with the world correspondingly, namely upper black and lower yellow. In the Han Dynasty, three features were represented in the ceremonial garment: upper coat with lower skirt, y-shaped collar and right-side knotting, bell-sleeves and wide waistband. Quju, a kind of lady's garment at that time was the most characteristic. It was a long, tight dress with spiral hem at the lower part. As China was a feudalist and hierarchical society, people had strong sense of family background. Accordingly, traditional Chinese garment also had sheer distinction between the casual and the formal occasions. In addition, anyone whether he or she was a close or remote relative to others or whether he or she was a noble or a humble person, a master or a servant could all be simply judged by the clothes. In general, the higher social position one had, the more elegant clothes one would wear. An important influence of such dressing custom on modern Chinese society is the ceremonial garment used in the funeral. The clothes of the dead person's close relatives are usually more complicated than the remote relatives'. Although silk was one of the earliest Chinese inventions, few people could afford it in ancient China. Its soft and undurable quality is now widely used in making pajamas or night gowns. Nowadays, the Chinese tunic suit and cheongsam are regarded as the classical gentleman and lady's social event's garments.

B. Chinese Opera

Chinese opera is a comprehensive, classical performing form. Different from western opera, it not only involves dialogue, monologue, singing, but also involves dancing, martial arts, acrobatics, and even mime. Each movement of the performer is carefully designed and the meaning that the movement expresses is also formularized. Even if for the Chinese native speakers, without systematic learning, they might not be able to easily comprehend it all. Actually, each local Chinese opera develops based on specific dialect region. In general, Kun opera is regarded as the oldest, most classical, and most difficult to comprehend in Chinese opera family. Peking opera is the most wide-spread one in China. The plots of Peking opera are mainly related to political and historical stories and it's very popular among the aged audience. The second wide-spread opera in China is Shaoxing opera which is mainly popular with the audience in Southeast China. It usually tells love stories of handsome young men and beautiful ladies. Nearly all the roles in Shaoxing Opera are performed by pretty actresses. Nowadays, the music of renovated Shaoxing opera uses modern instruments and sounds very fashionable and it is especially popular among female audience. The modeling of Chinese opera characters involves hair-dressing, facial make-up and costume-dressing. The make-up procedure and costume dressing of Chinese opera are very complicated. In most cases, performers need professional assistance to dress them up and they have to endure lots of physical pains. You won't believe that? Then just try it later.

Appendix D Course Assessment

考核方案一：适用于学生英文口语功底较好的班级

1. 总成绩 100 分 = 20% 期中口试 + 20% 期末口试 + 60% 平时成绩。
2. 口试成绩 = 完整性 25% + 准确性 25% + 流利性 25% + 互动性 25%。
3. 平时成绩 = 考勤纪律成绩（40 分）+ 小品表演成绩（20 分）+ 模拟导游成绩（20 分）+ 小组项目成绩（20 分）。
4. 考勤纪律 40 分：本学期共考勤 16 周，每周满分 2 分。一学期全部全勤且课堂表现良好者自动获得学期奖励加分 8 分。严重违反校规迟到、早退、旷课和严重违反课堂纪律者视情节轻重按项累计罚扣，罚分范围为每项 1—5 分。
5. 小品表演 20 分：每人每次最高 5 分。
6. 模拟导游讲解 20 分：每人每次最高 5 分。
7. 学期小组项目大作业（专题陈述）20 分，文字稿 10 分；报告表现 10 分。每组限选一题，全体组员都要参加文字稿的撰写与口头陈述。

考核方案二：适用于学生英文口语功底较一般的班级

1. 总成绩 100 分 = 20% 期中笔试 + 20% 期末笔试 + 60% 平时成绩。
2. 笔试成绩 = 旅游常用短语识记（10 分）+ 旅游专业词汇认知（30 分）+ 旅游专业常识判断（30 分）+ 旅游商务写作（15 分）+ 旅游专业文献翻译（15 分）。
3. 平时成绩 = 考勤纪律成绩（40 分）+ 小品表演成绩（20 分）+ 导游词口译成绩（20 分）+ 小组项目成绩（20 分）。
4. 考勤纪律 40 分：本学期共考勤 16 周，每周满分 2 分。一学期全部全勤且课堂表现良好者自动获得学期奖励加分 8 分。严重违反校规迟到、早退、旷课和严重违反课堂纪律者视情节轻重按项累计罚扣，罚分范围为每项 1—5 分。
5. 小品表演 20 分：每人每次最高 5 分。
6. 导游词口译 20 分：每人每次最高 5 分。
7. 学期小组项目大作业（专题陈述）20 分，文字稿 10 分；报告表现 10 分。每组限选一题，全体组员都要参加文字稿的撰写与口头陈述。

Student's Course Assessment Portfolio

Name			Student ID		
Week	Attendance & Discipline Credit Points	Fault Points	Exercise Performance	Credit Points	
1	2 points		Role-play 1	5 points	
2	2 points		Role-play 2	5 points	
3	2 points		Role-play 3	5 points	
4	2 points		Role-play 4	5 points	
5	2 points		Role-play 5	5 points	
6	2 points		Role-play 6	5 points	
7	2 points		Role-play 7	5 points	
8	2 points		Role-play 8	5 points	
9	2 points		Guiding 1	5 points	
10	2 points		Guiding 2	5 points	
11	2 points		Guiding 3	5 points	
12	2 points		Guiding 4	5 points	
13	2 points		Guiding 5	5 points	
14	2 points		Guiding 6	5 points	
15	2 points		Project Writing	10 points	
16	2 points		Presentation	10 points	
Mid-term: 20 points			Total		
Final Term: 20 points					
Course Tutor Signature:		Date:			

Bibliography

[1] 刘海霞. 旅游饭店职业英语. 北京：旅游教育出版社，2005.

[2] 孟君. 汉英旅游文物词典. 北京：旅游教育出版社，1998.

[3] 潘宝明. 中国旅游文化. 北京：旅游教育出版社，2005.

[4] 吴云. 旅游实践英语（上册）. 北京：旅游教育出版社，2007.

[5] 吴云. 旅游实践英语（下册）. 北京：旅游教育出版社，2007.

[6] 夏林根. 旅游目的地概述. 北京：旅游教育出版社，2005.

[7] 舆水优. 汉英中华文化图解词典. 上海：上海外语教育出版社，2000.

[8] 袁智敏，仉向明. 领队英语. 北京：旅游教育出版社，2005.

[9] 朱歧新，张秀桂. 英语导游翻译必读. 北京：中国旅游出版社，1999.

[10] DUBICKA I, O'KEEFFE M. 朗文旅游英语（初级）. 天津：南开大学出版社，2003.

[11] KRUSE B. 旅游业英语. 北京：外语教学与研究出版社，1997.

[12] HOLLOWAY J C. The Business of Tourism. 北京：外语教学与研究出版社，2004.

[13] JACOB M, STRUTT P. 朗文旅游英语（高级）. 天津：南开大学出版社，2003.

[14] PHP 研究所. 看图速记英语词汇集. 北京：外文出版社，1999.

[15] STRUTT P. 朗文旅游英语（中级）. 天津：南开大学出版社，2003.